RECIPES *from the*
TASTIEST, MESSIEST,

and MOST IRRESISTIBLE
FOOD TRUCKS

RECIPES *from the*
TASTIEST, MESSIEST,

and **MOST IRRESISTIBLE**
FOOD TRUCKS

JAMES CUNNINGHAM

PENGUIN

an imprint of Penguin Canada

Published by the Penguin Group

Penguin Group (Canada), 90 Eglinton Avenue East, Suite 700, Toronto, Ontario, Canada M4P 2Y3

Penguin Group (USA) Inc., 375 Hudson Street, New York, New York 10014, U.S.A.

Penguin Books Ltd, 80 Strand, London WC2R 0RL, England

Penguin Ireland, 25 St Stephen's Green, Dublin 2, Ireland (a division of Penguin Books Ltd)

Penguin Group (Australia), 707 Collins Street, Melbourne, Victoria 3008, Australia
(a division of Pearson Australia Group Pty Ltd)

Penguin Books India Pvt Ltd, 11 Community Centre, Panchsheel Park,
New Delhi – 110 017, India

Penguin Group (NZ), 67 Apollo Drive, Rosedale, Auckland 0632,
New Zealand (a division of Pearson New Zealand Ltd)

Penguin Books (South Africa) (Pty) Ltd, 24 Sturdee Avenue, Rosebank,
Johannesburg 2196, South Africa

Penguin Books Ltd, Registered Offices: 80 Strand, London WC2R 0RL, England

First published 2013

1 2 3 4 5 6 7 8 9 10 (C)

Library and Archives Canada Cataloguing in Publication

Cunningham, James
Eat St. / James Cunningham.

Includes index.
Based on the television program Eat St.
ISBN 978-0-14-318736-3

1. Street food. 2. Street-food vendors. 3. Cooking. 4. Eat St. (Television program). 5. Cookbooks.
I. Title. II. Title: Eat street. III. Title: Eat St. (Television program)

TX714.C86 2013 641.5 C2012-905172-1

American Library of Congress Cataloging in Publication data available

Visit the Penguin Canada website at www.penguin.ca

Special and corporate bulk purchase rates available; please see
www.penguin.ca/corporatesales or call 1-800-810-3104, ext. 2477.

CONTENTS

INTRODUCTION

Before I go any further, I must tell you that I am not a great cook. I am, however, a great lover of all foods and more accurately, the eating of them! I was backstage at a comedy club a while back when I received a call that would change my life . . . well, more accurately, my eating habits. The call was from a producer who was putting together a show about food trucks. He asked me if I would fly to New York City to film the pilot episode of *Eat St.* The rest, as they say, is history.

Before *Eat St.*, I had definitely indulged in my share of street food. As a standup comedian, I would often finish up at the clubs at two in the morning, when there aren't a lot of culinary options. At the time, my perception of "food truck" didn't go beyond the hotdog and fry carts that permeate our urban landscape.

But something really cool was starting to happen on the streets of Miami, Portland, Vancouver, New York, Toronto, Austin, Calgary, and dozens of other cities. The street food revolution was taking North America by storm and forever changing the way we looked at "street meat."

Everywhere, entrepreneurial chefs were converting old horse trailers, Winnebagos, buses, fire trucks, and of course the workhorse of the food truck industry, the Grumman, into mobile gourmet feast factories. Suddenly lobster rolls, Thai seafood curries, and Korean short rib tacos were replacing pretzels, fries, and dogs. Trucks were wrapped in glorious vinyl artwork, and the menus started looking like what you'd find at bricks-and-mortar restaurants. Lineups formed, first around the corner and then around the *block*! The food truck renaissance had begun.

But then things really started heating up. If there is one thing that the street food revolution can attribute its incredible and rapid success to, it is without a doubt social media. Now that almost everyone has a smartphone, food trucks

are able to connect with their customers twenty-four hours a day, wherever they are. Trucks can tweet their locations and stay in constant contact with their fans. Gone are the days of setting up somewhere and hoping patrons would show up—trucks are now opening to lineups. Social media has been so powerful, in fact, that there are menu items at some trucks that have more friends on Facebook than I do!

If you've ever eaten from a food truck, you know what a special culinary experience it is. People meet, talk, eat, share, form relationships—even get married—all in the name of *food*! It really is something magical, and that magic is what

we wanted to show you with *Eat St.*—a glimpse into these trucks and the lives and personalities of the people behind them (and *in* them!).

It has been a wild ride traveling all over North America and the U.K. to find "the most daring, delicious, and inventive street food around." Along the way we have not only made a lot of friends but experienced so much fabulous and exciting food that we just wouldn't find anywhere else.

Now, you may not have the opportunity to get down to Austin or out to Vancouver or over to Miami anytime soon, but

I'm sure you'd still like to taste the amazing food we feature on our show. In this book you'll find recipes for some of the most delicious things we have come across in our travels. Our friends on the trucks have divulged their secrets and offer you their recipes to try at home.

So invite some friends over, cook up a few dishes, and then turn on *Eat St.* for the total experience! The best part is you won't have to worry about getting a license, finding a good spot, firing up the generator, putting up the signage, and updating your Twitter feed—just sit back and enjoy!

James Cunningham

How do you like your

MOBILE
SNACKS

When you think of street food, it is impossible not to picture the fry truck. French fries are simply the most perfect street treat ever created. They are small, bite-size sticks of salty deliciousness that you can eat individually or by the handful. But why stop at fries? There are also the snacks on skewers, which all have something important in common—they are so easy to *share*. Stand near a food truck and the one thing you will hear over and over again is, "Oh my god, you have to try this!" After all, shareabilty is what makes street food street food!

This first chapter delves into fabulous fries, super snacks, and sensational skewers, the finest examples of portable perfection that we've found throughout our travels. And that's why we're sharing them with you…so that you can share them!

MOBILE SNACKS

THE FARRAH

Serves 4

When I first met Lani, Lisa, and Alana at the Fries and Dolls truck in Calgary, it is hard to say exactly what I fell in love with first. So overwhelming are their hot-pink truck and their sassy matching outfits, you forget temporarily that these gals dish out some of the best street food in North America. They have taken the concept of a fry truck to a new level with their own distinctive take on classic fried menu items.

The Farrah is one of the best french-fried creations I have ever tasted. It doesn't get better than a big cup of fresh-cut fries dusted with a delicious combination of herbs and chunks of garlic!

4 tsp (20 mL) olive oil
4 cloves garlic, chopped
Canola oil for deep-frying
2 lb (900 g) white potatoes, unpeeled, cut into medium-width french fries
¼ cup (60 mL) garlic oil (not roasted)
¼ cup (60 mL) chopped fresh parsley
¼ cup (60 mL) finely grated Grana Padano cheese
Pink Himalayan sea salt

In a small skillet over medium-high heat, heat olive oil. Add garlic and cook for 1 to 2 minutes. Garlic should still be firm but not browned. Transfer to a large bowl.

In a deep-fryer or deep, heavy saucepan, heat 2 inches (5 cm) of canola oil to 325°F (160°C). Working in batches, fry potatoes for 5 minutes. Drain on paper towels. Heat oil to 375°F (190°C). Fry potatoes a second time until golden and crispy. Drain on paper towels.

Stir 4 tsp (20 mL) of the garlic oil into sautéed garlic. Add french fries and drizzle with remaining garlic oil. Add parsley, Grana Padano, and sea salt to taste. Gently toss fries until evenly coated.

Spoon fries onto plates or into bowls and top with any garlic mixture left in the bowl.

NACHO GRANDE POUTINE

Serves 4

4 cups (1 L) chicken-based gravy

1⅓ cups (325 mL) chili

3½ lb (1.5 kg) Yukon Gold potatoes

Canola oil for deep-frying

Salt

1⅓ cups (325 mL) cheese curds, at room temperature

1⅓ cups (325 mL) tomato salsa

1 cup (250 mL) guacamole

1 cup (250 mL) sour cream

4 fresh or pickled jalapeño peppers, sliced

Heat gravy and chili separately until hot; keep warm.

Cut unpeeled potatoes into ½-inch (1 cm) sticks. Soak in cold water for at least 5 minutes.

In a deep-fryer or deep, heavy saucepan, heat 3 inches (8 cm) of canola oil to 300°F (150°C). Drain potatoes and pat dry. Fry for 4½ minutes, being careful not to brown potatoes. Drain on paper towels. Heat oil to 350°F (180°C). Fry potatoes until crispy and golden brown, about 2 minutes. Transfer to a large bowl lined with paper towels; season lightly with salt. Remove paper towels; gently toss potatoes.

Mound fries in serving dishes. Spread curds over fries. Pour hot gravy over curds. Mound chili over gravy; top with salsa. Spoon guacamole on the side. Serve garnished with a dollop of sour cream (or use a squeeze bottle) and jalapeño slices.

Poutine is a proud Canadian dish that combines all the heart-stopping power of melted cheese curds and gravy with the healthy benefits of a plate of deep-fried potatoes.

But even the deep-fried lovin' city of Toronto is not enough to contain the poutine army that Smoke is building. With a few restaurant locations already operational and a fleet of trucks planned across Canada and in the U.S., it won't be long before Smoke is at a street corner near you. To say these guys are passionate about poutine would be an understatement. They care so much that they oversee several fields in P.E.I. where they grow their own brand of "Smoke's potatoes"!

TROUBLE IN PARADISE

Serves 4

When you run a food truck in a city with more than four hundred other food trucks, it can be hard to stand out, but Chef Timber Anderson caught our eye because she's breaking all the rules with her truck. Whether you're looking for trouble or just an amazing twist on a classic hotdog, the Doghouse is the place to go in Portland. A Cordon Bleu chef who has been cooking since she was fifteen, Timber loves playing with food—right down to serving all her creations in actual dog dishes!

This dog recipe, with onions, pineapple, Pepper Jack cheese, and everybody's favorite, bacon, will be sure to get you out of the dog house.

Kicker Sauce

1 cup (250 mL) mayonnaise
¼ cup (60 mL) ketchup
2 tbsp (30 mL) whole-grain mustard
2 tbsp (30 mL) habanero sauce

Trouble in Paradise

3 lb (1.35 kg) frozen potato nuggets
Salt and pepper
1 tbsp (15 mL) canola oil
½ lb (225 g) bacon, chopped
1 cup (250 mL) pineapple chunks (fresh or drained canned)
½ cup (125 mL) chopped red onion
1½ cups (375 mL) shredded Pepper Jack cheese

For the Kicker Sauce, whisk together mayonnaise, ketchup, mustard, and habanero sauce until smooth. Refrigerate until needed.

Preheat oven to 450°F (230°C). Spread potato nuggets on a baking sheet and bake for 12 to 15 minutes, turning once, until golden brown. (Alternatively, deep-fry nuggets in a couple of inches of oil at 375°F/190°C for 3 to 5 minutes, until golden brown. Drain on paper towels.) Sprinkle nuggets with salt and pepper. Keep warm.

Meanwhile, heat a large skillet over medium heat. Add canola oil. Add bacon and cook, stirring occasionally, until bacon is half-cooked. Stir in pineapple and onion. Continue to cook, stirring frequently, until bacon is browned but not crisp. Spread onions, bacon, and pineapple into a thin, even layer, keeping ingredients close together. Top evenly with Pepper Jack cheese. Cook, without stirring, until cheese has melted.

Spread nuggets on a serving plate. Pour Kicker Sauce to taste over nuggets. Slide pineapple/cheese patty on top.

TRASHY CHORIZO AND CHIPS WITH FOIE GRAS

Serves 2

2 tbsp (30 mL) mayonnaise

2 tbsp (30 mL) plain yogurt

1 tsp (5 mL) whipping cream

½ tsp (2 mL) finely chopped parsley

¼ tsp (1 mL) minced garlic

Salt and pepper

2 large Yukon Gold potatoes

Canola oil for deep-frying

10 oz (280 g) Portuguese-style chorizo, sliced

3 oz (85 g) fresh foie gras

2 tbsp (30 mL) chopped fresh cilantro

2 tbsp (30 mL) chopped giardiniera (Italian pickled vegetables)

1 tbsp (15 mL) yellow curry powder

In a small bowl, combine mayonnaise, yogurt, cream, parsley, and garlic. Mix well. Season with salt and pepper. Set aside the garlic aïoli.

Using a mandoline or sharp knife, slice potatoes crosswise as thinly as possible. In a deep-fryer or deep, heavy saucepan, heat 2 inches (5 cm) of canola oil to 350°F (180°C). Working in batches if necessary, fry chips until golden brown. Drain on paper towels and sprinkle with salt.

In a large skillet over medium-high heat, fry chorizo until browned on both sides. Remove from pan and set aside.

Heat same skillet until very hot (just smoking). Score foie gras. Sprinkle with salt. Sear foie gras, scored side down, for 20 seconds. Flip and fry for another 20 seconds. Remove from pan and cut in two.

In a large bowl, gently toss together potato chips, chorizo, cilantro, giardiniera, a healthy dollop of garlic aïoli, and yellow curry, being careful not to break the chips too much. Divide between 2 plates and top with hot foie gras.

When Charles Thomas dropped out of art school and became a chef in a surf town in Portugal, he didn't think of himself as Eurotrash, but when he returned stateside, it turned out to be the perfect name for his Portland food truck. His customers are so glad he traded in his paint brush for a deep-fryer that they voted his Fishy Chips "Portland's favorite food cart dish" in 2010.

Trashy Chorizo and Chips with Foie Gras is the dish that really got our attention. This is gourmet street food at its best, a dish you simply won't find anywhere else. How Charles even *thought* of combining foie gras with french fries we'll never know, but you'll be glad he did!

KALBI CHUNK'D TOTS

Serves 4

One thing I love about street food is the number of chefs who combine several cooking traditions to create their dishes— a style known as fusion. One of the most remarkable examples we've come across is the Dim Ssäm à GoGo truck in Miami. Cracklin' Herb Duck and spicy Kimchi Grilled Cheese sandwiches are just two examples of the Asian/American/French dishes that Chef Richard Hales has invented. His truck has a huge following and is widely known as one of the most unique in the Miami area.

We all know how to make good ol' American tater tots—so why not combine them with Korean short ribs? Whammo! You're a fusion chef!

Kalbi Short Rib Marinade

1 cup (250 mL) soy sauce

2 tbsp (30 mL) sesame oil

1 tbsp (15 mL) minced ginger

1 tbsp (15 mL) minced garlic

1 tsp (5 mL) pepper

1 onion, sliced

1 apple, sliced

1 lb (450 g) Korean-style short ribs, ¼ inch (5 mm) thick

Cheese Sauce

1 cup (250 mL) shredded white Oaxaca, mozzarella, or other melting cheese

1 cup (250 mL) Korean red pepper paste

1 clove garlic

1 green onion, coarsely chopped

Kalbi Chunk'd Tots

Canola oil for deep-frying

1 lb (450 g) frozen potato nuggets

A pinch of sea salt

Chopped green onions

Hot sauce

Marinate the short ribs the day before. In a bowl whisk together soy sauce, sesame oil, ginger, garlic, pepper, onion, and apple. Add short ribs, turning to coat. Marinate, covered and refrigerated, overnight.

For the cheese sauce, in a food processor, combine cheese, red pepper paste, garlic, and green onions. Process until smooth, adding a little water if necessary to blend sauce. Set aside.

For the Kalbi Chunk'd Tots, preheat grill to high. Remove short ribs from marinade (discarding marinade). Grill short ribs until well done, turning once, about 3 minutes each side. Transfer to a cutting board and keep warm.

In a deep-fryer or deep, heavy saucepan, heat 2 inches (5 cm) of canola oil to 375°F (190°C). Working in batches if necessary, deep-fry potato nuggets until golden brown, 3 to 5 minutes.

With a slotted spoon, transfer nuggets to a large bowl. Toss with sea salt. Add cheese sauce and toss until coated. Transfer to a serving bowl.

Slice short ribs into bite-size pieces, discarding bones. Top nuggets with short rib meat, and serve garnished with green onions and hot sauce.

CHILI CHEESE FRIES

Serves 8

6 lb (2.7 kg) Kennebec or
    russet potatoes

2 large carrots

2 large stalks celery

1 onion

2 lb (900 g) ground beef

4 tsp (20 mL) salt

4 tsp (20 mL) black pepper

4 cloves garlic, minced

¾ cup (175 mL) tomato paste

2 tbsp (30 mL) chopped
    unsweetened dark chocolate

4 tsp (20 mL) sugar

4 tsp (20 mL) smoked paprika

2½ tsp (12 mL) ground cumin

2 tsp (10 mL) ground coriander

2 tsp (10 mL) dried Mexican oregano

2 tsp (10 mL) cayenne pepper

4 bay leaves

1 bottle (340 mL) dark lager

1½ cups (375 mL) water

4 tsp (20 mL) white vinegar

Canola oil for deep-frying

Shredded Cheddar cheese

Diced red onions for garnish

The day before, cut unpeeled potatoes into ¼-inch (5 mm) sticks. Soak in water overnight.

In a food processor, mince carrots, celery, and onion. Set aside.

Working in batches if necessary to avoid crowding the pan, place ground beef in a large pot. Season with salt and black pepper. Cook over medium heat until thoroughly browned. Transfer beef to a bowl and set aside. Cook carrots, celery, and onion in remaining fat, stirring occasionally, until soft. Stir in garlic; cook for 1 minute. Add browned beef, tomato paste, chocolate, sugar, paprika, cumin, coriander, oregano, cayenne, bay leaves, lager, water, and vinegar. Cook, stirring occasionally, for 30 minutes. Season to taste. Discard bay leaves. Keep warm.

Drain potatoes; dry well. In a deep-fryer or deep, heavy saucepan, heat 3 inches (8 cm) of canola oil to 325°F (160°C). Working in batches, fry potatoes for about 5 minutes—do not let them color. Drain on a rack. Heat oil to 400°F (200°C). In batches, fry potatoes until golden brown and crispy, 3 to 4 minutes. Drain on paper towels.

Divide french fries among serving bowls. Ladle chili over fries. Top with cheese and a sprinkle of red onion.

If you smell french fries for no apparent reason when walking around Los Angeles, you may have just passed the Frysmith truck. Erik Cho and his team have one of the most delicious and eco-friendly food trucks around. Not only do their fryers churn out some amazing food, but they recycle the oil to power their truck! This results in the most delicious and fragrant "drive-by" that you will ever have in L.A.

Beer, chocolate, beef, and onions in one dish? In the capable hands of the Frysmith, the result is magic. These are seriously tasty tubers!

SAIGON SHRIMP CEVICHE

Serves 4

Growing up in Santa Ana, Dos Chinos owners Hop Phan and Viet Tran were influenced by the Mexican and Asian cuisines all around them. Combining the two styles, they have created their own spin on dishes that are thrilling California foodies. Ceviche is a traditional way of preserving raw fish using lemon or lime juice. The juice's citric acid "cooks" the seafood, making it more firm and opaque just as though it had been cooked with heat. We found one of the best examples at Dos Chinos in Irvine, California.

This is one of the most popular dishes from the show. And what's not to love about a recipe that doesn't even require you to turn on your stove?

1 lb (450 g) headless medium shrimp, peeled and deveined

1 cup (250 mL) fresh lime juice (approx.)

⅓ cup (75 mL) sugar

½ cup (125 mL) fresh orange juice (from about 1 orange)

¼ cup (60 mL) tangerine juice (from about 1 large tangerine)

¼ cup (60 mL) fish sauce

1 to 2 habanero chilies, finely chopped

2 to 3 Thai bird's eye chilies, finely chopped

2 cups (500 mL) diced sweet red peppers (about 2 peppers)

2 cups (500 mL) diced cucumber

½ cup (250 mL) diced fresh pineapple

2 tbsp (30 mL) finely chopped fresh cilantro

½ red onion, finely chopped, for garnish

Finely chopped fresh parsley for garnish

Tortilla chips

Cut shrimp in half lengthwise and place in a nonaluminum bowl. Add lime juice; stir to make sure shrimp are well coated, adding more lime juice if necessary. Cover and refrigerate for 24 hours or until shrimp is pink and opaque.

Drain shrimp over a bowl, squeezing gently to remove excess lime juice. Return shrimp to bowl and return to refrigerator. Set aside ½ cup (125 mL) lime juice; discard remaining juice.

Add sugar to reserved lime juice; stir until you see a thin layer of sugar on the bottom of the mixture that won't dissolve completely. Stir in orange juice, tangerine juice, and fish sauce. Add habanero and Thai chilies to taste, sweet red peppers, cucumber, pineapple, and cilantro; stir well. Refrigerate for at least 1 hour.

Combine vegetable mixture with shrimp. Garnish with red onions and parsley. Serve with tortilla chips.

CHARBROILED OYSTERS

Serves 8 to 12

2 lb (900 g) butter, softened

½ cup (125 mL) finely chopped garlic

1 tbsp (15 mL) pepper

1 tsp (5 mL) dried oregano

6 dozen oysters on the half shell

1 cup (250 mL) mixed grated
    Parmesan and Romano cheese

3 tbsp (45 mL) chopped fresh parsley

In a medium bowl, blend butter with garlic, pepper, and oregano.

Preheat grill to high. Put oysters on the half shell right over the hottest part. Spoon enough seasoned butter over oysters so that some of it will overflow into the fire and flame up a bit.

Grill until oysters puff up and get curly on the sides. Remove from grill. Sprinkle with grated cheese and parsley. Serve immediately with hot French bread.

"Yum-yum, come get you some!" That is how the segment featuring Tommy Cvitanovich and his Drago's truck began, and it only got better from there. Tommy's truck wasn't just a food truck; it was a street party on wheels. For starters, it's a converted municipal fire truck that he altered to pump fluids he felt were more important than water: beer and Jägermeister. Only in New Orleans…

Though Tommy showed us how to make his famous jambalaya and crab cakes, here is his recipe for one of the most requested and tweeted-about dishes on *Eat St.* to date: Charbroiled Oysters. Fairly simple, but oh so good!

KOREAN BBQ PORK BELLY

Serves 6

Pork belly is the same portion of meat as bacon, so when purchasing your pork be sure to find a thick and meaty piece. You can find fresh pork belly at Asian markets.

I'm not a big fan of the fork, which is why I fell in love with Houston's Stick It. Ruth and Alberto had a great idea: why not take amazing gourmet concepts and serve everything up on sticks? If you're having a moving-in party or you recently had all your cutlery stolen, their dishes are perfect!

It's hard to believe neither of the creators are Korean once you taste their Asian-inspired BBQ pork belly. All you need are some bamboo skewers, some pork belly, and some basic spices.

3 cloves garlic, coarsely chopped
¼ cup (60 mL) soy sauce
3 tbsp (45 mL) dark brown sugar
2 tbsp (30 mL) sesame oil
1 tbsp (15 mL) rice wine vinegar or white vinegar
1 tsp (5 mL) chili oil
½ tsp (2 mL) hot pepper flakes
1 pork belly (1 lb/450 g), sliced into bacon-like strips
Sesame seeds and chopped green onions for garnish

In a medium bowl, combine garlic, soy sauce, sugar, sesame oil, vinegar, chili oil, and pepper flakes; whisk to dissolve sugar. Add sliced pork, turning to coat, and marinate, covered and refrigerated, for at least 8 hours or up to 24 hours.

Soak 12 bamboo skewers in cold water for at least 30 minutes before grilling.

Preheat grill to high.

Remove pork belly from marinade (discarding marinade). Thread pork onto skewers, weaving meat but keeping it as flat as possible. Grill skewers for 3 minutes per side. Watch closely while cooking—the oil from the marinade will cause the grill to flare.

Garnish with sesame seeds and chopped green onions. Serve with rice.

BEEF HEART SKEWERS

Serves 10

1 lb (450 g) fresh beef heart

½ cup (125 mL) extra-virgin olive oil,
   plus extra for drizzling

¼ cup (60 mL) sherry vinegar

2 tbsp (30 mL) whole-grain mustard

2 cloves garlic, minced

2 pinches of kosher salt

Coarsely ground pepper

Finely chopped fresh herbs for
   garnish (optional)

Soak 20 bamboo skewers in cold water for at least 30 minutes to help keep skewers from burning on the grill.

Trim beef heart of all veins, membranes, and excess fat. Cut into the longest strips possible, about ⅛ inch (3 mm) thick. Carefully thread heart pieces onto skewers, weaving meat but keeping it as flat as possible. Place skewers in a dish large enough to hold them in a single layer.

In a small bowl, whisk together oil, vinegar, mustard, garlic, salt, and pepper. Pour marinade over skewers. Let sit at room temperature for at least 10 minutes.

Preheat grill to highest heat. (Alternatively, heat a large cast-iron skillet or grill pan over high heat.) Grill heart skewers for 1 to 2 minutes per side, until grill marks show and meat is colored nicely. Serve warm, with a drizzle of olive oil and a sprinkling of fresh herbs (if using).

Many people dream of owning a food truck, but Chef Tony Adams's dream was to change the way his entire city ate. And at his Orlando food truck, Big Wheel Provisions, he is doing that one serving at a time. Tony is passionate about the ingredients that go into his recipes. All his dishes feature fresh, locally grown, organic vegetables, seafood, and meat. If that weren't enough, he also believes in "whole animal butchery," meaning he uses parts of the animal that other chefs usually throw out.

If you can, try to buy organic and local ingredients. You will taste the difference. Chef Tony claims that organic beef heart is as tender as filet mignon and, in his words, "tasty, tasty, *tasty!*"

THE ITALIAN LOLLIPOP

Serves 10

If there was one dish on *Eat St.* that made me want to install a commercial deep-fryer in my kitchen, it was this one. The Mangia Mangia truck in San Diego introduced us to Marko and Enzo, two of the most colorful characters we've ever had on the show. These amazing guys offered some phenomenal takes on classic Italian cuisine that blew us away, especially this one, with its simplicity and classic Italian flavor.

These lollipops will be the talk of your next party. As Marko says, "You dip it, you eat it, and then you love it!" Mangia mangia!

16 cups (4 L) marinara sauce

2 lb (900 g) ground meat mixture (40% beef, 40% veal, 20% pork recommended)

10 eggs

¾ cup (175 mL) grated Parmigiano-Reggiano cheese

¾ cup (175 mL) grated Pecorino Romano cheese, plus extra for dipping

3 tbsp (45 mL) dry Italian bread crumbs

2 tbsp (30 mL) dried oregano

2 tbsp (30 mL) chopped fresh flat-leaf parsley

2 tbsp (30 mL) pepper

4 tsp (20 mL) salt

1 tbsp (15 mL) canola oil, plus extra for deep-frying

1 pkg (10 oz/284 g) tempura mix

In a large pot, bring marinara sauce to a simmer.

In a large bowl, combine meat mixture, eggs, Parmigiano-Reggiano, Pecorino, bread crumbs, oregano, parsley, pepper, and salt. Mix well with your hands. Use a wet ice-cream scoop to make balls out of the mixture. Keep the scoop wet at all times so the meat does not stick to it.

Heat 1 tbsp (15 mL) canola oil in a large nonstick skillet over medium-high heat. Working in batches if necessary, fry meatballs for 3 minutes or until they are browned and get a nice crunchy coating. Using a slotted spoon, transfer meatballs to marinara sauce. Simmer, uncovered, for 40 minutes.

Put pot in the fridge to cool. When meatballs are cold, remove them from sauce.

In a deep-fryer or deep, heavy saucepan, heat 3 inches (8 cm) of canola oil to 375°F (190°C).

In a medium bowl, make tempura batter according to package instructions (the mixture should be about as thick as pancake batter). Put each meatball on a wooden stick. Dip balls in tempura batter, letting excess drip off. (Leftover tempura batter keeps, refrigerated, for up to 3 days.)

Deep-fry lollipops a few at a time until golden, 3 to 4 minutes. Dab them with paper towels, and sprinkle with salt. Serve with marinara sauce and pecorino cheese for dipping.

4 CHEEZY-MY-NEEZY

Serves 4

2½ cups (625 mL) warm water

1 tsp (5 mL) salt

2 cups (500 mL) precooked white cornmeal (arepa flour)

½ cup (125 mL) crumbled blue cheese

½ cup (125 mL) shredded Cheddar cheese

¼ cup (60 mL) shredded mozzarella cheese

¼ cup (60 mL) shredded provolone cheese

Vegetable oil for deep-frying

In a medium bowl, combine water and salt; stir to dissolve salt. Slowly stir in cornmeal. Knead until smooth. Knead in blue cheese, Cheddar, mozzarella, and provolone. Using your hands or an ice-cream scoop, form 1-inch (2.5 cm) balls.

In a deep-fryer or deep, heavy saucepan, heat 3 inches (8 cm) of vegetable oil to 375°F (190°C). Working in batches if necessary, fry cheese balls until golden brown, 1 to 2 minutes. Drain on paper towels. Serve with a spicy guava marmalade or a creamy cilantro garlic sauce.

When a chef says to you, "Food is a way of life," you know some good stuff is going to be coming out his serving window. So good, in fact, that that's what he called his truck: Mr. Good Stuff. And what Chef Alfredo Montero is known for all over Miami is stuffing his menu items with lots and lots of… well, good stuff!

Though most of Mr. Good Stuff's dishes feature the traditional arepa, a home-made corn tortilla/pita, we chose to feature some very easy-to-prepare cheese balls that are—you guessed it—stuffed with not one but four different cheeses!

"FRED & ETHEL" FISH SLIDERS

Serves 18 (with leftover slaw)

Lemon Crème Fraîche

1 cup (250 mL) crème fraîche
   or sour cream

1 tbsp (15 mL) whipping cream

1½ tsp (7 mL) lemon zest

1 tbsp (15 mL) lemon juice

Salt and pepper

Tropical Island Slaw

1 green cabbage, finely shredded

1 ripe but firm mango,
   peeled and diced

1 sweet red pepper, diced

Leaves from 1 bunch fresh
   cilantro, finely chopped

½ cup (125 mL) finely
   chopped red onion

½ cup (125 mL) lemon juice

Salt and black pepper

Sliders

5 lb (2.25 kg) skinless fish fillets
   (basa, tilapia, or halibut)

6 cloves garlic, minced

4 green onions, minced

Leaves from ¼ bunch fresh cilantro

2 serrano chilies, minced

1 tbsp (15 mL) smoked paprika

2 tsp (10 mL) sea salt

1 tsp (5 mL) freshly ground
   black pepper

⅓ cup (75 mL) olive oil

1 egg, lightly beaten

36 small brioche buns,
   halved horizontally

You don't have to know who Fred and Ethel were to appreciate these fish sliders. If you ever find yourself in San Jose and *don't* stop by the Babaloo truck, then "Lucy! You got some 'splainin' to do!"

Gladys Parada has brought to life not only the classic TV show but classic Cuban food that would make Ricky and Lucy proud. Maybe we're biased because we're on TV, but this popular duo has made our list of must-tries. Maybe this is the fine kettle of fish Ethel was always talking about!

For the crème fraîche, in a large nonaluminum bowl, combine crème fraîche, cream, lemon zest, and lemon juice; whisk until well blended. Season with salt and pepper. Cover and refrigerate until needed.

For the slaw, in a large bowl, combine cabbage, mango, red pepper, cilantro, and onion; toss. Add lemon juice and salt and black pepper to taste; toss well. Cover and refrigerate for at least 30 minutes to let flavors develop.

For the sliders, cut fish fillets in half lengthwise to facilitate feeding them through meat grinder. Grind fish through a meat grinder fitted with the medium plate into a large, nonaluminum bowl.

In a food processor, combine garlic, green onions, cilantro, and serrano chilies. Pulse until finely chopped. Add to ground fish. Add paprika, salt, and black pepper. Make a well in the center and pour in olive oil and beaten egg. Mix until thoroughly combined.

Line a baking sheet with parchment paper, then lightly oil paper. Using a small ice-cream scoop, shape fish mixture into 36 fish cakes. Arrange on baking sheet. Cover tightly with plastic wrap and refrigerate for at least 30 minutes to set.

Heat a griddle or cast-iron skillet over medium-high heat. Drizzle a little olive oil on the pan, and add fish cakes. Grill for 2 to 3 minutes per side, until golden brown.

Lightly toast cut sides of brioche buns on griddle. Spread cut sides with lemon crème fraîche. Top bottom half of each bun with a generous amount of tropical slaw, add a fish cake, and then the top bun. Use a long wooden pick to secure slider.

BUTTERMILK FRIED CHICKEN SLIDERS

Serves 3

Seasoning Blend

1 tsp (5 mL) garlic powder

1 tsp (5 mL) onion powder

1 tsp (5 mL) chili powder

1 tsp (5 mL) black pepper

1 tsp (5 mL) salt

½ tsp (2 mL) ground cumin

½ tsp (2 mL) ground coriander

½ tsp (2 mL) cayenne pepper

Sliders

2 tbsp (30 mL) seasoning blend

1 cup (250 mL) buttermilk

1 lb (450 g) boneless, skinless chicken breasts, cut into ½-inch (1 cm) pieces

2 large Yukon Gold potatoes, peeled

4 tbsp (60 mL) butter

¼ cup (60 mL) whipping cream

4 cloves roasted garlic

Salt and pepper

Oil for deep-frying

1 cup (250 mL) all-purpose flour

3 burger buns or kaiser rolls, halved horizontally and toasted

Country Gravy

½ cup (125 mL) butter

¼ cup (60 mL) all-purpose flour

4 cups (1 L) milk

½ tsp (2 mL) seasoning blend

For the seasoning blend, mix together garlic powder, onion powder, chili powder, black pepper, salt, cumin, coriander, and cayenne. (Seasoning blend keeps, in an airtight container, for several months.)

Start the sliders the day before. In a bowl whisk 1 tbsp (15 mL) of the seasoning blend into buttermilk. Add chicken. Cover and refrigerate overnight.

For the country gravy, melt butter in a medium saucepan over medium-low heat. Add flour; cook, whisking, until roux is golden and smooth, about 10 minutes. Whisk in milk. Cook, stirring, until thickened, about 10 minutes. Stir in seasoning blend. Add salt if needed. Keep warm.

Meanwhile, boil potatoes until tender, about 20 minutes. Drain and return to pot. Mash with potato masher; stir in butter, cream, and roasted garlic. Season with salt and pepper. Keep warm.

To finish sliders, in a deep-fryer or deep, heavy saucepan, heat 2 inches (5 cm) of oil to 350°F (180°C).

In a bowl, stir together flour and remaining 1 tbsp (15 mL) seasoning blend. Drain chicken (discarding buttermilk). Working in batches, dredge in seasoned flour. Deep-fry chicken until golden brown and cooked through, about 4 minutes, depending on thickness of chicken. Drain on paper towels.

Place mashed potatoes on bottom half of each bun. Place fried chicken on top and pour gravy over chicken. Top with top half of bun.

Nobody is rocking the slider and doing more exciting things with them than the crew at The Burnt Truck in Orange County. As Chef Paul Cao put it, "We wanted to keep it simple and reach into your inner seven-year-old and remind you of what you ate when you were younger." Menu items like the PBJ slider do just that.

So give yourself a break and let their luscious fried chicken sliders take you back to a time when your biggest worry was getting your homework done.

ROSEMARY PEANUTS AND BEETS WITH LEMON AND THYME

Serves 4

If you fall in love with this next dish, it's not a mistake. Truck owner Gail Lillian named her San Francisco truck LIBA because it means "love." In fact, printed on the side of the truck itself, she tells you to "Let your falafel affair begin."

But let's not even involve chickpeas at all. Let's do one of Liba's simplest and most delicious dishes. Guaranteed, it will send you head over heels. You can eat these beets on their own, but Lillian says they're more of a dressing to put on a salad or falafels. However you eat them, I guarantee they will *love* you back!

Rosemary Peanuts

3 tbsp (45 mL) fresh rosemary leaves

2 tbsp (30 mL) sugar

2 cups (500 mL) salted roasted peanuts

Beets with Lemon and Thyme

3 lb (1.35 kg) beets, trimmed

Zest of 1 lemon

Leaves from 1 bunch fresh lemon thyme or regular thyme, coarsely chopped

Salt

For the rosemary peanuts, finely chop rosemary. In a medium saucepan, combine rosemary and sugar. Add water until mixture has the consistency of wet sand. Simmer over low heat until sugar is dissolved and liquid is just starting to turn beige. Turn off heat. Add peanuts and stir rapidly until syrup coats nuts evenly. Cool peanuts in pan to allow syrup to harden.

For the beets, boil unpeeled beets until a fork penetrates easily, 30 minutes to 1 hour, depending on size. Drain beets, then cool under cold water. Refrigerate for at least 2 hours.

Wearing rubber gloves, slip skins off beets. Using a mandoline with a julienne blade, or a sharp knife, julienne beets. In a bowl, toss beets with rosemary peanuts, lemon zest, thyme, and salt to taste.

BEET HOME FRIES

Serves 8

20 medium beets, trimmed
½ cup (125 mL) vegetable oil
½ cup (125 mL) white vinegar
Soybean oil for deep-frying
2 cups (500 mL) cornstarch (approx.)

2 cups (500 mL) Japanese mayonnaise (such as Kewpie brand)
Shichimi togarashi (Japanese seven-spice blend)
½ cup (125 mL) sliced green onions

Preheat oven to 375°F (190°C).

Place a large sheet of foil on a baking sheet. Place unpeeled beets on foil. Drizzle with vegetable oil and vinegar. Place a second large sheet of foil over beets and crimp edges together to seal tightly. Roast for 2 hours or until tender.

Uncover beets and let sit until cool enough to handle. Wearing rubber gloves, slip skins off beets. Cut beets into 1-inch (2.5 cm) cubes. Chill.

In a deep-fryer or deep, heavy saucepan, heat 2 inches (5 cm) of soybean oil to 375°F (190°C).

Toss beets in cornstarch until evenly coated, adding more cornstarch if needed. Fry in 2-cup (500 mL) batches until cornstarch coating is crispy, 2 to 3 minutes.

Divide beets among 8 shallow bowls. Spoon about ¼ cup (60 mL) mayonnaise alongside each serving, and serve garnished with shichimi togarashi and green onions.

East Side King is a tiny trailer in Austin that knocked our socks off. They call their food Asian/bar-food fusion, and we couldn't believe the intense Japanese-inspired creations coming out the window. The long lines of patrons were kept happy as they listened to the musician on stage…who also happened to be the chef, Moto Utsunomiya!

East Side King usually sells out of their signature beet home fries by early evening. Let me tell you, if my mom had made beets with Japanese mayo and shichimi togarashi, I think I would have eaten them way more as a kid.

FRIED GREEN TOMATOES

Serves 4 to 6

A party in your mouth is one thing, but a party in your mouth out of a truck—now we're getting craaazy! The husband-and-wife team at Ibiza Bites hasn't copied a style of cooking, they've *invented* one. "SoLa," or Southern Latin American, is a blend of Jamie Morales's southern roots and Raf's (her hubby's) Venezuelan style.

No better example of SoLa is their adaptation of the classic southern staple fried green tomatoes. By deep-frying them with goat cheese and a panko coating and then adding a chipotle aïoli sauce, they've elevated a comfort food to a gourmet experience that is, well, a party in your mouth! As Jamie and Raf say, "Life is food. Taste life!"

Chipotle Aïoli

1 cup (250 mL) mayonnaise

2 chipotle chilies in adobo sauce, minced

1 tbsp (15 mL) lime juice

1 tsp (5 mL) honey

1 tsp (5 mL) soy sauce

½ tsp (2 mL) sesame oil

Fried Green Tomatoes

3 medium, firm green tomatoes

1 tbsp (15 mL) salt

1 egg

½ cup (125 mL) buttermilk

1 cup (250 mL) all-purpose flour

½ cup (125 mL) panko bread crumbs

½ cup (125 mL) peanut or vegetable oil

½ cup (125 mL) soft goat cheese

For the chipotle aïoli, in a medium bowl, whisk together mayonnaise, chilies, lime juice, honey, soy sauce, and sesame oil. Refrigerate until needed.

For the fried green tomatoes, cut tomatoes into ½-inch (1 cm) slices. Sprinkle both sides of tomatoes with salt. Let tomato stand for 5 minutes. Meanwhile, in a shallow dish, beat egg with buttermilk. Have ready in two separate dishes flour and panko crumbs. Lightly salt flour.

Heat oil in a large skillet over medium heat. Roll goat cheese into cherry-size balls. Press a goat cheese ball onto each tomato slice and spread evenly over tomato. Dip tomato slices in flour, then in egg mixture, letting excess drip off. Dredge slices in panko crumbs, coating thoroughly. Fry half the tomato slices at a time until brown, 3 to 5 minutes per side. Drain on a rack. Repeat with remaining tomato slices.

Serve drizzled with chipotle aïoli. Serve on a bed of stone-ground Cheddar grits, if desired.

BURGERS, DOGS & SLICES

Street meat—the burgs and dogs that have been the building blocks of our North American curbside food experience ever since the beginning. And is it even possible to walk a city block without passing at least one pizzeria? Let's face it, this is how we eat and this how we like it! But even though we consume millions of pounds of beef and dough every year, I guarantee you've never had *any* like the ones in this cookbook.

We love to find trucks and chefs that take classic food that we've all had before and add something special or prepare it a way that is just a bit different to create something that is out of this world. These recipes share those special little secrets that make this food so great.

BURGERS,
DOGS & SLICES

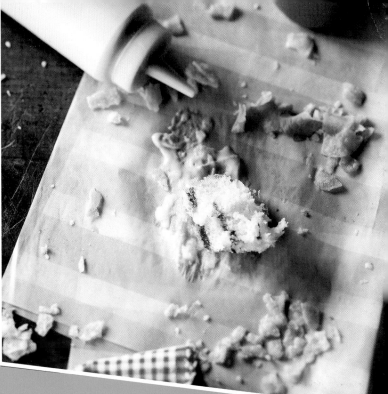

LATIN MACHO BURGER

Serves 6

To say you have the "world's *best* burger" is a big claim, but truck owner Jim Heins is originally from Texas, where everything is big. His Latin Macho Burger rules the streets of Miami, where it comes out of his pink-and-black tricked-out Latin Burger truck.

But there's a catch. A lot of the flavor in this burger can be attributed to the chorizo pork sausage, which makes up one-third of the blend along with chuck and top sirloin. So my question is, Is it a *burger* or is it a *sausage*? Either way, it's great… or as Jim would say, "Loco good!"

6 oz (170g) ground chuck
6 oz (170g) ground top sirloin
½ lb (225 g) fresh chorizo, casings removed
1 tbsp (15 mL) adobo seasoning
1 large onion, grated
1 tbsp (15 mL) olive oil
2 large onions, thinly sliced

Salt and black pepper
½ cup (125 mL) minced jalapeño peppers
½ cup (125 mL) dark brown sugar
2 roasted red peppers
¾ cup (175 mL) mayonnaise
6 potato rolls, halved horizontally
6 slices white American cheese

In a large bowl, thoroughly combine ground beef, chorizo, adobo seasoning, and grated onion. Shape into 6 patties. Refrigerate for at least 30 minutes, until firm.

Meanwhile, heat olive oil in a large skillet over medium-high heat. Add sliced onions; season with salt and black pepper. Add jalapeños and brown sugar. Sauté for 15 minutes or until onions are caramelized and soft. Remove from heat and set aside.

In a food processor, combine roasted red peppers, mayonnaise, and salt and pepper to taste. Process until well combined and creamy.

Preheat grill to high. Grill burgers until cooked to desired doneness.

Spread 1 tbsp (15 mL) red pepper mayonnaise on cut sides of each roll. Lay a burger on the bottom half and top with caramelized onions, a cheese slice, and top half of roll.

THE YELLOW SUBMARINE | *Miami, Florida*
YELLOW BURGER

Serves 4

½ can (14 oz/398 mL) crushed pineapple in heavy syrup

2 lb (900 g) ground chuck

Ground cumin

Salt

Black pepper

4 burger buns

4 slices provolone cheese

Lettuce leaves

4 slices tomato

4 slices onion

Mustard, ketchup, and coarsely crushed potato chips for garnish

In a medium saucepan, bring crushed pineapple to a boil, then let cool. Purée in a blender.

Preheat grill to high.

Using your hands, mix beef with cumin, salt, and black pepper to taste. Shape into 4 patties. Grill patties for about 4 minutes per side.

Toast cut sides of burger buns on grill. Put a burger on the bottom half of each bun; top each with 1 slice of provolone, lettuce, tomato, onion, some crushed pineapple, mustard, ketchup, and crushed potato chips.

We just had to find out the secret ingredients that make the Yellow Burger so different from any other we have ever tasted on the show. Andreas, Flavio, and Angela, the brothers-and-sister team that own Miami's Yellow Submarine truck, were nice enough to give us the recipe, which their mother created for them.

The flavor surprise is a mixture of pineapple sauce, provolone cheese, and crushed potato chips—a sweet-tart-creamy-crunchy combo. I guarantee you've never tasted a burger like this before!

THE NUT BURGER

Serves 2

You've heard of punk music, but punk burgers? Sean Sullivan loves the zombie look of his Manhattan truck as much as the Frankenstein creations going out his window. He and his chefs will boldly declare, "No one is doing what we're doing." And they're right!

You would think that smearing peanut butter on the bottom of a brioche bun would be enough to make the burger experience unique. But there is *so* much more that goes into the burgers at Feed Your Hole. After hanging out with these fun guys for a while, it's easy to forget they have some serious gourmet chops. Give this one a try and feed *your* hole!

½ lb (225 g) center-cut bacon
1 tsp (5 mL) salted butter
½ lb (225 g) ground brisket
¼ lb (115 g) ground top sirloin
¼ lb (115 g) ground chuck

Coarse sea salt
1 tsp (5 mL) extra-virgin olive oil
½ cup (125 mL) peanut butter
2 brioche buns, halved horizontally

Chop bacon into small pieces. Melt butter in a nonstick skillet over medium heat. Add bacon and cook to desired doneness. Set aside.

Using your hands, gently but thoroughly mix brisket, sirloin, and chuck. Shape into 2 patties. Season both sides with sea salt.

Heat a large cast-iron skillet over medium-high heat. Coat with olive oil; heat until hot but not smoking. Add burgers and cook for 4 to 5 minutes per side for medium doneness. Remove from pan and sprinkle with coarse sea salt.

Spread 2 tbsp (30 mL) peanut butter on cut sides of each bun. Divide bacon between top halves of buns. Top bottom halves with a burger, close buns, and wait a minute before serving so the peanut butter melts.

THE WHOLE TRUCK BURGER

Serves 3

Portuguese Aïoli

1 tbsp (15 mL) mayonnaise

1 tsp (5 mL) piri-piri sauce

Burgers

¾ lb (340 g) ground Angus chuck

Kosher salt and black pepper

4 oz (115 g) cheese curds

3 organic free-range eggs

12 slices bacon

3 sesame burger buns

3 leaves lettuce

6 slices heirloom tomato

9 slices dill pickles

15 slices jalapeño pepper

6 thin slices red onion

For the Portuguese aïoli, stir together mayonnaise and piri-piri sauce. Refrigerate until needed.

For the burgers, preheat grill to high.

Season beef with salt and pepper and shape into 3 patties. Grill patties to desired doneness. Top burgers with cheese curds during final minute or so of cooking.

While burgers are cooking, fry eggs sunny-side up on grill, cook bacon to desired crispness on grill, and toast buns on grill.

Place burgers on bottom halves of buns. Top each burger with 1 egg, 4 slices bacon, 1 lettuce leaf, 2 slices tomato, 3 slices pickle, 5 slices jalapeño, 2 slices onion, and 1 tsp (5 mL) aïoli.

On certain nights of the week, the five-star Char-cut steakhouse in Calgary would offer up burgers made from their prime Alberta beef leftovers "speakeasy style," in the back alley behind the kitchen. Problem was, the lineups out the back alley were soon longer than the lineups at the front door. It was time to take the crowds elsewhere. The solution? A food truck! And so Alley Burger was born.

It takes no stretch of the imagination to understand why this burger is called the Whole Truck Burger. It's got practically everything in the whole truck in it!

HAWAIIAN BULGOGI BURGER

Serves 6

A Hawaiian burger from a Mexican/Korean fusion truck? That is the kind of thing that is right up our alley on *Eat St.* The guys at Chi'Lantro combine tacos and traditional Mexican fare with Korean favorites like kimchi and ginger sauce, all in all making the street foodies of Austin very pleased.

Where's the beef? Oh, it's here, but it's not the traditional patty we're used to. This is bulgogi, baby—traditional Korean marinated beef, combined with melted cheese (on the grill, please, to hold the beef together), and then the toppings. We've all had pineapple on pizza before, but on a burger it is beyond!

Korean Bulgogi
1 onion, finely chopped
2 tbsp (30 mL) minced garlic
1 tsp (5 mL) minced ginger
¾ cup + 2 tbsp (200 mL) soy sauce
¼ cup (60 mL) sugar
2 tbsp (30 mL) vinegar
2 tsp (10 mL) sesame oil
2 lb (900 g) thinly sliced
    rib-eye steak

Spicy Mayo
2 tbsp (30 mL) sriracha sauce
1 tbsp (15 mL) shichimi powder
1 cup (250 mL) mayonnaise

Garnishes
Thickly sliced onion
6 pineapple rings
Shredded Cheddar Jack cheese
Shredded Monterey Jack cheese
6 sesame burger buns
Thinly sliced green leaf lettuce
Thinly sliced napa cabbage
Sliced tomatoes

For the bulgogi, in a food processor, combine onion, garlic, ginger, soy sauce, sugar, vinegar, and sesame oil. Process until onion is finely minced. Place rib-eye in a resealable plastic bag and add marinade. Marinate, refrigerated, turning once or twice, for 24 hours.

For the spicy mayo, whisk sriracha and shichimi powder into mayonnaise. Refrigerate until needed.

Preheat flattop grill or griddle to high. Remove rib-eye from marinade (discarding marinade). Grill until nearly desired doneness, turning once. Meanwhile, grill onions and pineapple rings next to meat until lightly charred. Push meat and onions into 6 portions. Sprinkle with Cheddar Jack and Monterey Jack. (The melting cheese holds the meat and onions together like a patty.) Meanwhile, toast buns.

Divide lettuce and cabbage among bottom halves of toasted buns. Top with patties. Garnish with grilled pineapple rings and tomatoes.

MIGHTY MASALA FISH BURGER

Serves 6

Fish Burgers

2-inch (1 cm) piece fresh ginger, peeled and minced

1 whole head garlic, minced

2 tbsp (30 mL) garam masala

2 tbsp (30 mL) paprika

1 tbsp (15 mL) hot pepper flakes

2 tsp (10 mL) chili powder

2 tsp (10 mL) ground cumin

2 tsp (10 mL) coriander seeds

1 tsp (5 mL) turmeric

½ tsp (2 mL) fennel seeds

1 tbsp (15 mL) sugar

1 tbsp (15 mL) salt

2 lb (900 g) thick skinless coley, pollack, or cod fillets, cut in 6 portions

1 tbsp (15 mL) vegetable oil

Mint Cumin Raita

1 cup (250 mL) plain yogurt

1 tbsp (15 mL) mint sauce

1 tsp (5 mL) ground cumin

1 tsp (5 mL) finely chopped fresh mint

Salad

1 tsp (5 mL) sweet tamarind paste

1 tsp (5 mL) chaat masala

Juice of 1 lime

1 onion, finely chopped

1 cucumber, finely chopped

2 ripe tomatoes, finely chopped

Leaves from 1 bunch fresh cilantro, coarsely chopped

For serving

6 khubz (Middle Eastern flatbreads) or large pitas, warmed

Mango chutney

Indian pickles

Taste, fusion, and *delight*— the three words that make up the philosophy of Alec Owen and his Bhangra Burger bus in London, England. The bus itself is a converted old horse truck lovingly named Baba Gupta Bhangra, and out of it flows goodwill, peace, and some of the best burgers you've ever tasted. Flavoring locally sourced meats and seafood with spices and rubs he discovered on many trips to India, Alec claims to be blending the very best of the West and the East.

The Mighty Masala Fish Burger could well be the best Indian-inspired fillet-o-fish you will ever come across, in a restaurant or on the street.

For the fish burgers, using a mortar and pestle, crush ginger, garlic, spices, sugar, and salt to a paste. Add a little oil if needed for a spreadable consistency. Cover fish all over with the paste. Wrap each portion in plastic wrap and refrigerate for 24 to 48 hours.

For the mint cumin raita, in a small bowl stir together yogurt, mint sauce, cumin, and fresh mint until well mixed. Refrigerate until needed.

For the salad, in a small bowl, whisk together tamarind paste, chaat masala, and lime juice. In a large bowl, combine onion, cucumber, tomatoes, and cilantro. Add dressing; toss to coat.

In a large skillet, heat vegetable oil over medium heat. Fry fish for 3 to 5 minutes per side, depending on thickness. Fish will flake easily when done and be opaque inside.

Serve fish wrapped in flatbread with the salad, mango chutney, Indian pickles, and mint cumin raita.

TERIMAYO DOG

Serves 4

Folks in Vancouver will tell you Japadog is the cart that started the street food revolution. Foodies come from all over the planet to have Chef Noriki Tamura's dogs. I don't consider a trip to Vancouver complete without consuming at least three of the delicious doggies. Noriki came to Vancouver to open a restaurant, but due to budgetary constraints went with a cart. At the time the city would only issue him a permit to serve hotdogs, so he got creative and came up with what must be the best Asian fusion hotdog stand in the *world*! Noriki is truly one of the first celebrity street chefs.

You'll notice that we feature not one but two recipes in the book, simply because we had the same dilemma everyone has when standing in front of the Japadog menu—you can never have just one!

1 tbsp (15 mL) butter
2 onions, sliced
4 kurobuta pork or other sausages, briefly boiled

4 hotdog buns
Teriyaki sauce
Japanese mayonnaise (such as Kewpie brand), in a squeeze bottle
Dried seaweed, cut into thin strips

Spiritually prepare yourself by imagining that you are the world's top sushi chef. Close your eyes for 1 minute, relax, and keep telling yourself that you can do it!

When you are ready, melt butter in a large skillet over medium-high heat. Add onions and cook, stirring frequently, until slightly browned. Remove from heat and keep warm.

Preheat grill to medium-high. Grill sausages, turning, until cooked through but still juicy. Meanwhile, toast buns.

Place sausages in buns. Place fried onions in a line the length of each sausage. Sprinkle sausages with enough teriyaki sauce to cover, making sure sauce covers both tips of the sausage so the first bite has lots of flavor. Squeeze thin lines of Japanese mayonnaise at a 45-degree angle to sausages and along length of sausages. Pile seaweed on top of sausages. Make sure you smile while making the Terimayos Dogs.

OROSHI DOG

Serves 4

4 bratwurst or other sausages

4 hotdog buns

1 cup (250 mL) oroshi
   (grated daikon radish)

Thinly sliced green onions

Usukuchi (light) soy sauce

Spiritually prepare yourself by imagining that you are a samurai. Become one. Concentrate for 5 minutes on combining the humble Japanese culture with the power of America.

Prepare bratwurst sausage by grilling at medium-high heat. Sausage should be grilled until fairly cooked. Meanwhile, toast buns.

Place sausages in buns. Place a thin layer of oroshi over each sausage, covering entire surface of sausage. Sprinkle with green onions. Sprinkle with soy sauce, so covering most of the oroshi. Make sure you smile while making the Oroshi Dogs.

No longer do you have to make your way to Vancouver to experience Japadog like we did. Japadog has such a good thing going on that they expanded to New York. So, lucky you if you live in Manhattan or are thinking of visiting the Big Apple.

Chef Noriki Tamura created two special versions of his dog recipes just for this book, so we just had to include both of them for you to try. Who doesn't love a good dog? Chef, you are the best!

THE DOGFATHER

Serves 4 (with leftover marinara sauce)

Roasted Red Pepper Marinara Sauce

2 tbsp (30 mL) olive oil

1 small onion, finely chopped

1 small carrot, finely chopped

½ stalk celery, finely chopped

½ tsp (2 mL) finely chopped garlic

1 tsp (5 mL) hot pepper flakes

1 tsp (5 mL) black pepper

½ tsp (2 mL) salt

2 tbsp (30 mL) red wine

2 tsp (10 mL) cornstarch

2 tsp (10 mL) brown sugar

2 tsp (10 mL) tomato paste

1 can (19 oz/540 mL) peeled tomatoes, puréed

1 jar (14 oz/398 mL) roasted red peppers, drained and finely chopped

The Dogfather

4 hotdog buns

4 all-beef hotdogs

2 large white onions, sliced and grilled

1 tbsp (15 mL) dried oregano

8 oz (225 g) mozzarella cheese, cubed

½ cup (125 mL) finely chopped red jalapeño peppers

7 oz (200 g) cured chorizo, sliced

½ cup (125 mL) grated Parmesan cheese

Americans eat 20 billion hotdogs a year. The British eat…considerably fewer. So to find an amazing hotdog vendor in the streets of London is a find indeed. When we went across the pond to check out street food in Jolly Old, the locals quickly directed us toward South London to see Cooper Deville, aka the Dogfather.

This self-styled classic is a meal in itself. Onions, chorizo sausage, mozzarella, oregano…interested yet? I thought so.

For the marinara sauce, heat oil in a large saucepan over medium heat. Add onion, carrot, celery, garlic, pepper flakes, black pepper, and salt; cook until vegetables are soft and cooked through. Remove from heat. Using an immersion blender, blend vegetables into a paste. Stir in wine, cornstarch, sugar, and tomato paste. Return pot to medium-high heat and cook, stirring constantly, for 5 minutes. Add tomatoes and roasted red peppers; bring just to a boil. Turn heat down to very low and simmer, uncovered and stirring frequently, for 90 minutes.

For the Dogfather, heat a large skillet over medium heat. Slice open hotdog buns and place cut sides down in skillet until toasted. Meanwhile, boil or grill hotdogs until heated through. Set aside hotdogs and buns, keeping warm.

In same skillet over medium heat, make 4 piles with onions; sprinkle with oregano. Press mozzarella cubes into onions; heat through until cheese begins to melt. Spread open hotdog buns and spread a pile of onion/mozzarella mixture on bottom half of each bun. Top with jalapeños.

In same skillet, heat chorizo until the oils in the chorizo start to sizzle. Arrange chorizo on top half of each bun. Place a hotdog in each bun; top each hotdog with a spoonful of roasted red pepper marinara sauce; sprinkle generously with Parmesan.

HOT SOUTHERN MESS

Serves 10

Pimento Cheese

¾ cup (175 mL) mayonnaise

½ jar (7 oz/207 mL) diced pimentos, drained

1 tbsp (15 mL) granulated garlic

Pinch of cayenne pepper

Salt and black pepper

4 cups (1 L) shredded white Cheddar cheese

Slaw

6 tbsp (90 mL) mayonnaise

4 tsp (20 mL) white vinegar

2 tbsp (30 mL) sugar

½ tsp (2 mL) celery salt

½ tsp (2 mL) salt

¼ tsp (1 mL) pepper

1 small green cabbage, shredded

For each serving

1 all-beef hotdog

1 hotdog bun

2 tbsp (30 mL) hot Tennessee chow-chow relish

This dish is a delicious hot southern mess, coming straight from Nashville's only self-proclaimed "full-service Weenery." When Leslie Allen hung up her lab coat and left her chemistry degree behind, she took the next logical step. She converted a VW camper van into a food truck that makes hotdog lovers' dreams come true.

What sets this dog apart is chow-chow, a Tennessee sweet relish with hot sauce, peppers, and tomatoes that will make any doggie bark. Mess up your kitchen with this one!

Make the pimento cheese and the slaw the day before. For the pimento cheese, in a large bowl, combine mayonnaise, pimentos, garlic, cayenne, and salt and black pepper to taste. Stir together well. Add cheese and mix thoroughly. Refrigerate for several hours or overnight for best flavor.

For the slaw, in a large bowl, whisk together mayonnaise, vinegar, sugar, celery salt, salt, and pepper until smooth. Add cabbage and mix well. Refrigerate overnight.

For each serving, grill hotdog. Heat hotdog bun. Top hotdog with 2 tbsp (30 mL) pimento cheese, 2 tbsp (30 mL) slaw, and 2 tbsp (30 mL) chow-chow.

THE 7TH INNING STRETCH

Serves 4

4 jumbo spicy hotdogs

4 naan, each about
    6 inches (15 cm) long

½ cup (125 mL) creamy peanut butter

4 tbsp (60 mL) sweet-and-spicy
    barbecue sauce

1⅓ cups (325 mL) shredded
    smoked Gouda cheese

6 slices bacon, cooked
    until crisp, crumbled

1 cup (250 mL) caramel popcorn
    (such as Cracker Jack)

Preheat grill to medium. Grill hotdogs, turning, until heated through and skins are browning a bit, about 4 minutes. A minute or so before hotdogs are ready, sprinkle naan with water and heat on grill for a few minutes, flipping bread to make sure it is warm on both sides and folds easily. Remove from grill.

In a microwave or small pot, melt peanut butter. Top each naan with a hotdog. Drizzle 2 tbsp (30 mL) peanut butter over each hotdog, thoroughly covering them. Drizzle 1 tbsp (15 mL) barbecue sauce over peanut butter; peanut butter and barbecue sauce should blend together. Sprinkle hotdogs with Gouda, bacon, and caramel popcorn. Wrap naan around hotdogs and secure with a toothpick.

When you first see the hotdogs at the Short Leash trailer in Phoenix, your initial thought might be: "Why didn't I think of that!" I was so completely blown away by the simplicity of what they were doing, I can't believe there aren't a thousand trucks doing the same thing.

Forget the twenty-four toppings like mango chutney, jalapeños, and blue cheese. For owners Brad and Kat, it's all about the bun—or lack thereof. Almost all Short Leash dogs are served wrapped in fresh Indian naan bread, making them more of a wrap than a dog. But who cares what they're called when they taste out of this world!

NEAPOLITAN THIN-CRUST PIZZA

Makes four 14-inch (35 cm) pizzas

When a portable-pizza-oven concept goes from a single stove to three full-time locations and a bricks-and-mortar restaurant, you know that pizza has gotta be good! Veraci Pizza appeared on the Seattle scene back when owners Marshall and Erinn left their jobs with a mission to create the most delicious ultra-thin artisanal crust in Washington State. Sourcing their ingredients locally and using ovens that cook each pizza in about two minutes, their pies are simply to die for.

This recipe might look complicated, but trust me, it's a perfect example of "simpler is better."

2 cups (500 mL) warm water (100°F/38°C)
½ tsp (2 mL) active dry yeast
1 tsp (5 mL) turbinado or other raw cane sugar
5 cups (1.25 L) unbleached all-purpose flour
1 tsp (5 mL) sea salt

1 tbsp (15 mL) olive oil
Tomato sauce
Cheeses of choice, including shredded mozzarella
Additional toppings (precooked meats or raw vegetables)
Finely chopped fresh parsley
Dried Italian herbs

Remove top rack from oven (to allow for more space) and place a pizza stone (if using) on lower rack. Preheat oven to 550°F (290°C) for at least 30 minutes.

Pour warm water into a large bowl. Whisk in yeast and sugar. Whisk in 4 cups (1 L) of the flour, 1 cup (250 mL) at a time, blending thoroughly after each addition. Dough should be very thick and lump-free.

Mound remaining 1 cup (250 mL) flour on work surface. With your hand, make a well in the center, leaving some flour on the bottom. With a rubber spatula, transfer dough to flour. Using the heel of your hand, slowly knead flour and dough together. Scrape under dough with a dough scraper and add more flour underneath as necessary to keep dough from sticking. Knead dough until it is no longer loose or sticky. Knead in salt. Continue kneading dough for 3 minutes.

Cut dough in half and examine the interior; if dough is too soft, the "wall" will slump down. In this case, continue kneading and slowly add a little more flour. Dough is ready when the interior wall remains upright. (If too much flour is added, dough will become unworkable.)

Cut dough into 4 equal portions and shape each into a ball. Lightly coat a baking sheet with olive oil. Place dough balls on it and lightly brush each ball with oil. Cover dough with plastic wrap or a kitchen towel and let rest (proof) at room temperature for 20 to 30 minutes.

To shape the pizza, roll out 1 dough ball on a floured surface with a rolling pin, sprinkling with a little flour on top of dough if needed to keep it

from sticking. Keep flipping pizza "skin" over and over as you roll it. The crust will get thinner and thinner. Fix any holes by pinching the dough back together.

When dough is about 14 inches (35 cm) wide, rub a very thin layer of flour across top of skin, then flip dough over and onto a wooden peel. (If you do not have a peel, flip dough onto a lightly oiled rimless baking sheet.) Shake peel to make sure skin slides easily. If not, add a little more flour and repeat.

Dress pizza with a thin layer of tomato sauce, leaving a 1-inch (2.5 cm) border (the *cornicione,* or crust) at outer edge. Distribute a light layer of your favorite cheeses, including mozzarella, on top. Add additional toppings—the fewer, the better. Sprinkle pizza with a pinch of parsley and dried Italian herbs. Carefully pat down toppings so they won't slide around, and test-shake pizza to make sure it will slide off the peel.

Slide pizza onto preheated pizza stone, shaking peel slightly to release pizza (or transfer baking sheet to oven). Bake for 8 to 15 minutes or until *cornicione* is golden brown. Remove pizza with peel and let cool for a minute or two before cutting and serving.

Repeat with remaining dough balls. (Wrap unused dough tightly in plastic wrap and refrigerate for up to 3 days or freeze for up to 3 months.)

BIANCA PIZZA

Makes four 8-inch (20 cm) pizzas

Pizza Dough

1 lb (450 g) all-purpose flour

1 pkg instant yeast

1 tbsp (15 mL) kosher salt

1 tsp (5 mL) sugar

1¼ cups (300 mL) warm water
 (about 105°F/40°C)

2 tbsp (30 mL) olive oil

Pepper

Toppings

½ cup (125 mL) mascarpone cheese

1 tsp (5 mL) porcini powder

1 tbsp (15 mL) dried oregano

2 oz (55 g) provolone cheese,
 thinly sliced

2 oz (55 g) Gorgonzola cheese,
 thinly sliced

2 oz (55 g) Manchego cheese,
 thinly sliced

2 oz (55 g) Brie cheese, thinly sliced

4 tsp (20 mL) ground toasted
 pistachios

1 cup (250 mL) lightly packed
 baby arugula

1 tsp (5 mL) white truffle oil

2 oz (55 g) Parmigiano-Reggiano
 cheese, grated

Start the pizza dough the day before. Combine flour and yeast in the bowl of a stand mixer fitted with the dough hook. Add salt, sugar, water, and olive oil. Mix on low speed until dough comes together, about 3 minutes. Increase speed to medium and knead for 15 minutes.

Fold dough onto itself and shape into a smooth ball. Put dough in a large oiled bowl and turn to coat with oil. Cover with plastic wrap and leave at room temperature to double in size, about 1 hour. Refrigerate overnight. Let stand at room temperature for 1 hour before using.

Turn dough out onto a work surface and cut into 4 equal portions. Flatten each piece into a disk; lightly brush with oil. Let rest on work surface, uncovered, for 30 minutes.

Preheat grill to high. Oil grill grates and lower heat to medium.

Using your hands, stretch and flatten 1 dough disk until very thin. Season both sides with salt and pepper. Grill dough, covered, for 30 seconds, until grill marks show. Flip dough and grill for another 30 seconds, until grill marks show. Using tongs, transfer crust to a baking sheet. Repeat.

Lower grill temperature to very low. Evenly spread mascarpone over each pizza crust, leaving a 1-inch (2.5 cm) border. Dust with porcini powder and oregano. Arrange provolone, Gorgonzola, Manchego, and Brie over pizzas. Slide pizzas from sheet onto grill, close lid, and grill until cheese is melted and crust is golden brown underneath and very crispy, about 2 minutes.

Transfer to a cutting board. Evenly top with pistachios and arugula. Drizzle with truffle oil and sprinkle with Parmesan.

It's hard to say what's most impressive about Chef Joe Youkhan. His size? His black and purple belts in kung-fu and jujitsu? His many culinary awards? For us it is his Orange County food truck, the Tasting Spoon. From a man who does things in a big way, our favorite dish is, oddly enough, a simple one.

The Bianca Pizza at first doesn't seem to pay enough homage to the many years Joe spent as a chef and restaurateur…until you taste it. There are six cheeses here and that has to add up to one of the best pizzas you've ever tasted!

PESTO CHICKEN PIZZA

Makes one 16-inch (40 cm) pizza

Tom and Eric would be the first to tell you there's nothing fancy schmancy about the pies coming out of DC Slices. This ex-T-shirt vendor and ex-air traffic controller know the most important rule of gourmet Italian: less is a-more. They tried fancy crusts and toppings, but they found success in simplicity. Like Tom says, "We're just two guys trying to make pizza." Both Democrats and Republicans agree that this is the best mobile pizzeria in Washington—even if it is the only one!

When you make the Pesto Chicken Pizza, remember their motto: "It's not a DC slice unless you use the spice."

Pizza Dough

1 cup (250 mL) warm water (100°F/38°C)
1 pkg active dry yeast
½ tsp (2 mL) sugar
3½ cups (875 mL) bread flour
1 tsp (5 mL) sea salt
1½ tsp (7 mL) olive oil

Pesto Chicken Pizza

¾ cup + 2 tbsp (200 mL) pesto
1 cup (250 mL) shredded mozzarella cheese
½ lb (225 g) cooked chicken breast, chopped
Chopped fresh basil

For the pizza dough, place warm water in a small bowl; stir in yeast and sugar until dissolved. Cover bowl and set aside until liquid is foamy, about 10 minutes.

In a large bowl, combine 3 cups (750 mL) of the flour with salt. Make a well in the center and add yeast mixture and oil. Beat with a wooden spoon to form a soft, sticky mass.

Turn dough out onto a well-floured work surface. With floured hands, knead dough, adding more flour, a little at a time, until smooth and elastic, 8 to 12 minutes. Shape dough into a ball. Place dough in a large oiled bowl, turning to coat with oil. Cover with wax paper and a clean kitchen towel, and let dough rise in a warm place until doubled, about 1 hour.

With a floured fist, punch down dough. Cover again and let rise for another 40 minutes.

Meanwhile, preheat oven to 425°F (220°C). Lightly oil a 16-inch (40 cm) pizza pan or screen, or a rimless baking sheet.

For the pizza, on a lightly floured work surface, roll out dough to a 16-inch (40 cm) circle. Fit dough into pizza pan. Spread pesto over dough, leaving a ½-inch (1 cm) border. Sprinkle cheese evenly over pizza. Arrange chopped chicken over cheese.

Bake pizza for 25 to 30 minutes, until crust is golden and cheese is bubbling. Let stand for 5 minutes (if you can wait that long). Sprinkle with basil, then slice and serve.

ULTIMATE STREET
SANDWICHES

John Montagu, the fourth earl of Sandwich, had a problem back in 1765. He found that it was nearly impossible to eat a meal during a lengthy card game while staying focused on his cards. Little did he know that the food item that bears his name to this day would be celebrated in the streets. From the deli rolls of New York to the tortas of Mexico, the sandwich is the ultimate handheld food. And when the kitchen it comes out of is mobile, well, my friends, you're looking at a sandwich that's the best thing since sliced bread!

Don't let the term sandwich fool you, though. Most of the recipes in this chapter are full meals. Many may seem a bit more involved than your everyday sandwich, but they are easy to eat . . . and to looove.

ULTIMATE STREET SANDWICHES

AVOCADO MELT

Serves 4 (with leftover pesto)

Arugula Walnut Pesto

½ cup (125 mL) walnuts

Zest and juice of 1 lemon

2 cloves garlic

½ cup (125 mL) grated Parmesan cheese

2 lb (900 g) arugula

½ cup (125 mL) basil leaves

1 cup (250 mL) olive oil

Salt and pepper

Sandwiches

8 thick slices whole wheat bread

8 slices Swiss cheese

2 avocados, sliced

Crisp bacon (optional)

For the pesto, in a food processor combine walnuts, lemon zest, garlic, and Parmesan; process until smooth. Add arugula, basil, olive oil, lemon juice, and salt and pepper to taste; process until smooth, adding a little water if necessary for desired consistency. (Pesto keeps, covered and refrigerated, for up to 1 week.)

For the sandwiches, heat a griddle or large skillet over medium heat. Smear pesto on one side of each slice of bread. Top bread with Swiss cheese. Place bread on griddle and tent loosely with foil (or cover skillet). Cook until bottom is toasted and cheese melts. Remove from pan. Arrange avocado and bacon on 4 slices. Close sandwiches and serve.

The great thing about having a mobile food truck is that you can stop off at local farms along your way and pick up the freshest produce and meats. That isn't quite what San Diego food truck owners Kari and Dave Rich do with their truck, FoodFarm, but it's pretty close. Everything used at FoodFarm comes from local organic purveyors, and the Riches pride themselves on using only sustainable ingredients.

This Avocado Melt is not at all what you expect when you hear "grilled cheese." Until you try it, and then that'll be all you can think about! The creamy melted cheese and avocado on the inside are contrasted by the crunchy bread on the outside. Both Kari and Dave call it their "official" favorite sandwich.

VEGGIE MELT

Serves 8

The truck that started it all! Michelle and Dave's Grilled Cheese Truck was the very first truck we featured on *Eat St.* I still remember being blown away by the fact that in a given day, this truck goes through eighteen hundred slices of bread and fifty pounds of cheese!

The Veggie Melt is one of the most popular they serve, keeping the street food aficionados of Los Angeles very happy indeed. But don't let the word *veggie* fool you into thinking this is some kind of health-smart choice. To make the butter spread, you have to whip it with mayonnaise... oh so good!

½ cup (125 mL) balsamic vinegar
¾ cup (175 mL) butter, at room temperature
¾ cup (175 mL) mayonnaise
16 slices whole-grain bread

32 thin slices Gruyère or Swiss cheese
4 cups (1 L) baby arugula
4 cups (1 L) sliced fresh strawberries
2⅔ cups (650 mL) fennel sliced paper thin

Boil balsamic vinegar in a small saucepan until reduced to ¼ cup (60 mL), about 5 minutes. Let syrup cool.

In a stand mixer fitted with the paddle attachment, beat butter and mayonnaise until thoroughly blended, scraping down sides of bowl several times.

Preheat griddle to 350°F (180°C) or heat a large skillet over medium heat.

Generously spread butter mixture on one side of each slice of bread, spreading right to the edges. Turn 8 slices buttered side down. Top each with 2 slices Gruyère, ½ cup (125 mL) arugula, ½ cup (125 mL) straw-berries, and ⅓ cup (75 mL) shaved fennel. Drizzle with 1½ tsp (7 mL) balsamic syrup. Top with 2 slices Gruyère. Top with remaining bread, buttered side up.

Grill sandwiches until golden brown on the bottom. Carefully flip and continue to cook until bottom is golden brown and cheese is melted. If bread browns before filling is hot, transfer pan with sandwiches to a 450°F (230°C) oven to finish.

CRAB AND BRIE GRILLED CHEESE

Serves 2

1 cup (250 mL) fresh
   Dungeness crabmeat

2 tbsp (30 mL) mayonnaise

Zest and juice of 1 lemon

1 tbsp (15 mL) chopped chives

4 dashes of hot pepper sauce

4 thick slices artisanal bread

¼ cup (60 mL) mascarpone cheese

¼ cup (60 mL) shredded sharp
   Cheddar cheese

1 tomato, finely chopped

¼ cup (60 mL) sliced cucumber

4 thick slices Brie cheese

¼ cup (60 mL) mango chutney

2 tbsp (30 mL) butter

Cracked pepper

Lemon wedges for garnish

Preheat oven to 350°F (180°C).

In a small bowl stir together crabmeat, mayonnaise, lemon zest and juice, chives, and hot pepper sauce.

Spread 2 slices of bread with mascarpone. Sprinkle with Cheddar. Top with crab mixture. Scatter tomato over crab. Top with sliced cucumber. Arrange Brie over cucumber. Spread mango chutney evenly on remaining 2 slices of bread. Close sandwiches.

In a large ovenproof nonstick skillet over medium-low heat, melt butter until foaming. Place sandwiches in pan and cook until bottom is toasted, about 2 minutes. Flip sandwiches and transfer pan to oven; bake for 4 minutes or until a melting tenderness is reached. Serve sandwiches sprinkled with cracked pepper and garnished with lemon wedges.

Chefs Andrew Gruel and Jethro Naude had a great idea when they started their truck SlapFish in the City of Angels. They offered locally caught seafood and dealt directly with the fishermen. Because of this they were able to offer high-quality seafood at fast-food prices, a formula that made their truck so popular, they shut it down!

But don't worry. They swapped their four wheels for two bricks-and-mortar locations, and now you can enjoy their signature Lobsticles or Crab and Brie Grilled Cheese while sitting down. In case you can't make it to Orange County anytime soon, though, now you can enjoy the Crab and Brie sitting down in your very own bricks-and-mortar location.

TRIPLE-CREAM BRIE MELT

Serves 2

"There is no food that doesn't improve when you add cheese to it." That is the mantra of chef and owner James Klayman of New York's Gorilla Cheese truck—and he's right! Tired of his life as a New York real estate broker, James hung up his suit to pursue a higher calling: he dedicated his life to cheese.

For proof of his mantra, look no further than his creation the Triple-Cream Brie Melt. This baby contains strawberry jam and—wait for it—prosciutto. If cheese makes so-so food taste great, imagine what will happen with *this* combination!

4 slices triple-crème Brie,
  ¼ inch (5 mm) thick
4 thick slices French bread, cut on the
  diagonal
2 generous tbsp (40 mL)
  strawberry preserves
8 thin slices prosciutto
Butter, softened

Heat a panini press until hot.

Arrange Brie on 2 slices of the bread. Spread strawberry preserves over cheese; top with prosciutto. Close sandwiches. Brush both sides with butter. Cook sandwiches in panini press for 3 minutes or until golden brown. (Or grill in skillet over medium heat, pressing down with spatula and turning once, about 5 minutes.)

PIMENTO MAC AND CHEESE

Serves 4

1 clove garlic, chopped

1 tsp (5 mL) cayenne pepper

1 tsp (5 mL) paprika

1 tsp (5 mL) kosher salt

1 tsp (5 mL) black pepper

1 tsp (5 mL) hot pepper sauce

1 cup (250 mL) mayonnaise

½ cup (125 mL) shredded
    mild yellow Cheddar cheese

1½ cups (375 mL) shredded smoked
    Cheddar cheese

1 cup (250 mL) cooked and cooled
    macaroni

1 small roasted red pepper, diced

8 slices bread, buttered generously
    on one side

1 tomato, sliced

4 slices bacon, cooked and crumbled

In a food processor, combine garlic, cayenne, paprika, salt, black pepper, and hot sauce. Pulse briefly to mix. Add mayonnaise, yellow Cheddar, and ½ cup (125 mL) of the smoked Cheddar. Pulse until combined. Transfer mixture to a bowl and fold in cooked macaroni and roasted red pepper.

Heat a nonstick griddle to 300°F (150°C) or a large nonstick skillet over medium heat. Arrange 4 slices of bread, buttered side down. Top each slice with 1 cup (250 mL) mac and cheese mixture, 2 slices tomato, a quarter of the bacon, and ¼ cup (60 mL) of the remaining smoked Cheddar. Top with remaining slices of bread, buttered side up. Grill sandwiches until golden brown on both sides, about 5 minutes.

Why have one of your favorite comfort foods when you can have two—in one sandwich! The Grilled Cheeserie in Nashville is taking grilled cheese to the next level thanks to gourmet chef Crystal Bogan. In her words, "For a chef, cheese is like a blank canvas. Flavors just go so well with it." And pretty much *any* cheese. Crystal uses everything from Colby Jack to queso fresco to homemade pimento cheese in her creations.

The Grilled Cheeserie serves up most sandwiches with tomato soup for dipping—a combination that will take you right back to your childhood.

CHICKPEA SANDWICH

Serves 6

Chickpea Patties
1½ cups (375 mL) chickpea flour
1½ tsp (7 mL) salt
½ tsp (2 mL) black pepper
½ tsp (2 mL) ground cumin
¼ tsp (1 mL) cayenne pepper
2½ cups (625 mL) water
¼ cup (60 mL) chopped fresh flat-leaf
    parsley

Lemon Aïoli
5 cloves garlic
1½ tsp (7 mL) Dijon mustard
Zest and juice of 1 lemon
3 egg yolks
1½ cups (375 mL) light olive oil (or
    canola/olive oil blend)

Slaw
6 radishes, thinly sliced
3 cups (750 mL) shredded carrots

4 tsp (20 mL) rice wine vinegar
4 tsp (20 mL) extra-virgin olive oil
Salt and pepper

Sandwiches
1 delicata squash or small butternut
    squash
Vegetable oil for deep-frying
6 ciabatta buns, halved horizontally
Olive oil for brushing
4 cups (1 L) mixed salad greens

If Tony Soprano had moved to Portland, this would have been his favorite food cart: classic New Jersey Italian street food, but done West Coast style with locally sourced produce and meat. When Chef Kevin Sandri reluctantly introduced burgers on his menu, they became so popular that he changed his focus, closed down Garden State, and opened a new truck called Burgatroyd.

We had to include one of the Garden State creations to give you a taste of the amazing things Sandri was doing with chickpeas.

For the chickpea patties, lightly oil a 12- × 8-inch (30 × 20 cm) baking sheet. In a medium, heavy saucepan, whisk together chickpea flour, salt, black pepper, cumin, and cayenne. Slowly add water, stirring with a wooden spatula until mixture is smooth (a few lumps are okay). Stir constantly over high heat until mixture begins to thicken, then lower heat as mixture continues to thicken. When most of the water has been absorbed, add parsley. Continue to stir until chickpea mixture is thick and pulls away from the sides and bottom of the pot, 10 to 15 minutes. Spread mixture evenly in baking sheet. (If desired, oil the bottom of another baking sheet and place it on top of chickpea mixture. Press firmly to create a smooth, even surface, then remove.) Cool completely. (Meanwhile, make aïoli and slaw and roast squash.)

For the aïoli, in a food processor combine garlic, mustard, lemon zest and juice, and egg yolks; purée. With motor running, drizzle in olive oil until mixture is thick like mayonnaise. Refrigerate until needed.

For the slaw, in a bowl toss together radishes, carrots, vinegar, oil, and salt and pepper to taste. Set aside at room temperature.

To roast the squash, preheat oven to 350°F (180°C). Peel butternut squash if using. Cut squash in half lengthwise and remove seeds, then cut crosswise into ¼-inch (5 mm) slices. Toss with a little olive oil and a pinch of pepper, spread on a baking sheet, and bake until easily pierced with a knife, 10 to 15 minutes. Keep warm.

For the sandwiches, in a deep-fryer or deep, heavy saucepan, heat 2 inches (5 cm) of vegetable oil to 350°F (180°C). Cut chickpea mixture into 12 pieces. Working in batches, fry patties until crispy and beginning to brown, about 4 minutes. Drain on paper towels and sprinkle lightly with salt. (Alternatively, bake patties in a 400°F/200°C oven for about 25 minutes, or grill for about 3 minutes per side.)

Lightly brush cut sides of buns with olive oil; toast cut sides on a grill or under a broiler. Spread aïoli on each cut side. Divide salad greens among buns. Top with slaw, then place 3 or 4 slices of roasted squash on top. Top each sandwich with 2 patties and close sandwiches.

MAINE LOBSTER ROLL

Serves 4

2 live lobsters (each 1½ lb/675 g)
½ cup (125 mL) butter

4 brioche hotdog buns, sides trimmed
⅓ cup (75 mL) chopped celery

Bring a large pot of water to a boil. Add lobsters, cover, and cook for 12 minutes. Cool lobsters under cold running water. Remove all meat from lobsters. Chop meat into generous chunks; set aside.

Melt 1 tbsp (15 mL) of the butter in a large skillet over medium heat. Toast sides of the buns until light brown. Remove buns from pan.

Add remaining 3 tbsp (45 mL) butter, celery, and lobster meat to the pan. Heat gently, stirring, until warmed through, 1 to 2 minutes. Be careful not to overcook the mixture or the lobster will lose its moisture. Divide mixture among buns.

Sam's ChowderMobile offers up the best East Coast seafood—even though Sam is not on the East Coast at all. Based in Half Moon Bay, California, Sam is the guy who flies in seafood daily from Maine and serves it up in a variety of chowders and tacos. He'll even throw you and twenty friends a private clambake under the Golden Gate Bridge!

Before hosting *Eat St.*, I had never had a true East Coast lobster roll. I don't know what it is about this amazing creation, but if you're a seafood lover, you have to drop whatever you're doing right now and try this.

CATFISH PO' BOY

Serves 4

Fried Catfish

4 skinless catfish fillets
   (about 3 lb/1.35 kg)
4 cups (1 L) buttermilk
4 cups (1 L) cornmeal
2 tsp (10 mL) salt
Black pepper
White pepper
Cayenne pepper
Paprika
Garlic powder
Onion powder
Peanut oil for deep-frying

Coleslaw

1 green cabbage, finely chopped or
   thinly sliced
2 bunches green onions, thinly sliced
2 jalapeño peppers, seeded if desired
   and finely chopped
1½ cups (375 mL) mayonnaise
Dash of cider vinegar
Pinch of garlic powder
Black pepper

Rémoulade Sauce

1 cup (250 mL) mayonnaise
1 tbsp (15 mL) whole-grain mustard
2 tsp (10 mL) finely chopped onion
1 tsp (5 mL) cayenne pepper
½ tsp (2 mL) chipotle hot sauce
6 dashes of hot pepper sauce
Squeeze of ketchup
Small squeeze of lemon juice
Generous pour of olive oil
Garlic powder

Sandwiches

2 or 3 fresh tomatoes, sliced
4 small French loaves
   (or 2 baguettes, halved
   crosswise), halved horizontally

In season 2 we met the cutest couple north of the Mason-Dixon Line in, of all places, Brooklyn. Jen Catron and Paul Outlaw have brought true southern cooking to the city, and there is no better example of what they're all about than their Catfish Po' Boy. Delicious, generous, spicy, and *big*! This is what y'all call down-home cookin'. Yee-haw!

For the fried catfish, soak catfish in buttermilk, covered and refrigerated, for at least 3 hours. (Meanwhile, make coleslaw and rémoulade sauce.)

For the coleslaw, in a large bowl, combine cabbage, green onions, and jalapeños. In a small bowl, stir together mayonnaise, vinegar, garlic powder, and black pepper to taste. Add half of mayo mixture to vegetables and toss to coat; add more mayo mixture until coleslaw reaches desired sauciness. Refrigerate until needed.

For the rémoulade sauce, in a small bowl, whisk together mayonnaise, mustard, onion, cayenne, chipotle hot sauce, hot pepper sauce, ketchup, lemon juice, olive oil, and garlic powder to taste. Refrigerate until needed.

To finish the catfish, in a bowl, toss cornmeal with salt and spices to taste until mixture begins to darken in color and is well seasoned. For a spicier catfish fry, be generous with the cayenne. Working with 1 fillet at a time, dredge fillets in cornmeal mixture until well coated.

In a deep-fryer or cast-iron Dutch oven, heat 3 inches (8 cm) peanut oil to 350°F (180°C). Working in batches if necessary, deep-fry fillets, turning once, until deep golden and crispy, 6 to 10 minutes. Drain on paper towels.

To finish the sandwiches, place tomato slices on bottom halves of bread. Spoon coleslaw liberally over tomatoes. Place catfish on top. Spoon rémoulade sauce liberally over fish. Cover with top halves of bread.

PORK MEATBALL BANH MI

Serves 4

Pickled Vegetables

1 cup (250 mL) rice wine vinegar

1 cup (250 mL) water

¼ cup (60 mL) sugar

1 tbsp (15 mL) salt

1 lb (450 g) carrots, julienned

1 lb (450 g) daikon radish, julienned

Sriracha Mayo

1 cup (250 mL) mayonnaise

¼ tsp (1 mL) sesame oil

Sriracha sauce

Meatballs

1 lb (450 g) ground pork

1 tbsp (15 mL) salt

1 tbsp (15 mL) sugar

1 tbsp (15 mL) sriracha sauce

1 tbsp (15 mL) fish sauce

1 bunch green onions, chopped

1 egg, lightly beaten

¼ cup (60 mL) panko
    bread crumbs (approx.)

Banh Mi

4 small French loaves or
    ciabatta buns,
    halved horizontally

1 bunch fresh cilantro,
    tough stems discarded

Make the pickled vegetables the day before. Bring vinegar, water, sugar, and salt to a boil. Remove from heat. Place carrots and radish in a non-aluminum bowl; pour hot liquid over top. Let cool to room temperature. Cover and refrigerate overnight. Drain before using.

For the sriracha mayo, in a small bowl, stir together mayonnaise and sesame oil. Stir in sriracha sauce to taste. Refrigerate until needed.

For the meatballs, preheat oven to 350°F (180°C). In a large bowl, combine ground pork, salt, sugar, sriracha sauce, fish sauce, green onions, and egg. Using your hands, mix gently but thoroughly. Mix in only enough panko crumbs to bind mixture without making it dry or heavy. With damp hands or a damp ice-cream scoop, make 12 meatballs.

Heat a large ovenproof nonstick skillet over medium-high heat. Sear meatballs until golden brown on all sides. Transfer pan to oven and bake for 20 minutes, or until a meat thermometer inserted in the center of a meatball reads 160°F (70°C).

For the banh mi, toast cut sides of bread. Spread sriracha mayo on both cut sides. Place 3 warm meatballs in each sandwich. Top with a generous amount of drained pickled vegetables. Place a generous amount of cilantro on top. Close sandwiches.

Just to look at Lardo, you'd think it was a quaint little cottage on wheels serving up delicious meat menu items from its happy little food truck pod in Portland. But once you *tried* their food, you'd realize it was actually a *shrine* dedicated to the creation of magnificent pork sandwiches.

This cart was so successful that Chef Rick Gencarelli went bricks-and-mortar, expanding the concept into a sandwich shop and beer garden. The locals are loving it. You might say the Portlandians are pigging out!

ZORBA BALLWICH

Serves 7

Tzatziki

1 cup (250 mL) Greek-style
    plain yogurt
½ cup (125 mL) sour cream
½ cup (125 mL) finely
    chopped fresh dill
1 tsp (2 mL) lemon juice
1 tsp (2 mL) pepper
Salt
1 cucumber, finely chopped

Tomato Olive Spread

1 cup (250 mL) crushed tomatoes
¼ to ½ cup (60 to 125 mL) finely
    chopped pitted Kalamata olives

2 tbsp (30 mL) extra-virgin olive oil
2 tbsp (30 mL) red wine vinegar

Lamb Meatballs

1 small egg
¼ cup (60 mL) crumbled feta cheese
¼ cup (60 mL) panko bread crumbs
¼ cup (60 mL) buttermilk
1½ cloves garlic, minced
¼ cup (60 mL) finely
    chopped fresh mint
2 tbsp (30 mL) finely
    chopped fresh parsley
½ tsp (2 mL) lemon zest

Pinch of lamb seasoning
Pinch of Greek seasoning
Pinch of beef bouillon powder
Pinch of salt
1 lb (450 g) ground lamb

Sandwiches

7 soft rolls, halved horizontally
1 large butter or romaine lettuce,
    chopped
3 cups (750 mL) crumbled
    feta cheese
2 medium red onions, chopped
1½ cups (375 mL) chopped fresh mint
Dried oregano

Haulin Balls claims to have the best meatballs in Vegas, and after trying almost every one of them we have to agree.

The Zorba is the truck's take on a Mediterranean gyro but in ballwich form: lamb meatballs with a tomato-olive spread and tzatziki in a soft roll. I guarantee you will have a ball making it!

For the tzatziki, in a medium bowl, whisk together yogurt, sour cream, dill, lemon juice, pepper, and salt to taste. Stir in cucumber. Adjust seasoning. Refrigerate until needed.

For the tomato olive spread, stir together tomatoes and olives. Stir in oil and vinegar until well mixed. Set aside.

For the meatballs, preheat oven to 400°F (200°C). In a large bowl, beat egg. Stir in feta, panko crumbs, and buttermilk until well mixed. In a small bowl, stir together garlic, mint, parsley, lemon zest, lamb seasoning, Greek seasoning, bouillon powder, and salt. Add to panko mixture and mix thoroughly by hand. Add lamb; mix by hand until blended evenly. Shape into balls about 1½ inches (4 cm) in diameter (you should have at least 21 balls). Transfer to a baking dish. Bake until cooked through but still moist, about 30 minutes.

For the sandwiches, spread one side of each roll with tzatziki and the other side with tomato olive spread. Arrange chopped lettuce on bottom half of rolls. Top with 3 meatballs. Top meatballs with feta, chopped red onion, fresh mint, and a sprinkling of dried oregano. Close sandwiches.

WHAT ZANE EATS SANDWICH

Serves 4

Elinor's Chopped Liver

1 lb (450 g) beef liver, cleaned of outer skin and veins

Salt and pepper

½ cup (125 mL) schmaltz (rendered chicken fat), melted

1 cup (250 mL) sliced onions

1 hard-cooked egg

Sandwiches

20 slices salami, ¼-inch (5 mm) thick

8 slices double-rye bread

1 cup (250 mL) thinly sliced red onions

½ cup (125 mL) Russian honey mustard

4 sour pickles

For the chopped liver, preheat oven to 350°F (180°C). Cut liver into 1-inch (2.5 cm) chunks; sprinkle with salt and pepper. Arrange in one layer in a baking dish. Bake for 40 minutes or until liver is cooked through but still a little pink in the middle.

Meanwhile, in a large skillet over medium heat, heat 2 tbsp (30 mL) of the schmaltz. Add onions; cook, stirring frequently, until caramelized, about 1 hour.

In a food processor, combine liver and egg; process until smooth. With motor running, drizzle in remaining schmaltz until well combined. Transfer to a bowl. Stir in caramelized onions and salt and pepper to taste.

For the sandwiches, grill or fry salami. Smear 4 bread slices with chopped liver. Top with salami, then sliced red onions. Drizzle with mustard. Close sandwiches, pressing slightly so they ooze mustard, fat, and liver. Serve with sour pickles.

If you've ever wondered what Zane Caplansky looks like, you only have to walk up to his truck, known around the streets of Toronto as Thunderin' Thelma. Painted in large renaissance reality is his smug mug in classic deli stance. Immediately you know this food truck is going to be different— and fun!

Zane calls his cuisine "Jewish soul food," and if you want to know what the man himself eats, here it is! Chopped liver, salami, mustard, and chicken fat. This guy is my Jewish soul brother from another mother!

CAPRESE

Serves 4

Don't be fooled by the Jalopy's name—there is nothing broken or run-down about it. This converted 2001 Freightliner FL80 is so big, the sandwiches have to be sent down on a slide to street level. Why would someone want such a big truck? So that he had enough room for a rotisserie oven, of course! The delicious, juicy chicken that makes up most of the sandwiches here is brined overnight and slow-roasted in its own juices.

The Caprese is one of the Jalopy's specialties, and they know they've made it right if you have juice running down your arm. Chef Nic Patrizi says a sandwich isn't done right unless it's messy. And I totally agree.

Pesto

Leaves from 2 bunches flat-leaf parsley, chopped

Leaves from 1 sprig fresh thyme, chopped

Leaves from 1 sprig fresh oregano, chopped

4 cloves garlic, chopped

Zest of ½ lemon

1 tbsp (15 mL) lemon juice

1 tbsp (15 mL) cracked black pepper

1 tsp (5 mL) toasted coriander seeds

⅔ cup (150 mL) olive oil

Salt

Parsley Salad

2 tbsp (30 mL) finely chopped parsley

1 tsp (5 mL) finely chopped green onion

¼ tsp (1 mL) finely chopped garlic

Black pepper

Sandwiches

8 thick slices French or sourdough bread

¼ cup (60 mL) sliced fresh mozzarella

1 to 2 ripe heirloom tomatoes, sliced

1½ cups (375 mL) shredded rotisserie chicken

For the pesto, in a blender, combine parsley, thyme, oregano, garlic, lemon zest, lemon juice, pepper, and coriander seeds; blend just until mixture is finely chopped. With motor running, drizzle in olive oil. Season with salt.

For the parsley salad, in a small bowl combine parsley, green onion, garlic, and pepper to taste.

For the sandwiches, heat a griddle or large skillet over medium heat. Lightly brush with olive oil. Place 4 slices bread on griddle. Arrange mozzarella on bread. Top with parsley salad, tomato slices, chicken, and pesto to taste. Cook for about 5 minutes, until mozzarella is melted and bread is toasted. Meanwhile, toast remaining 4 slices of bread. Close sandwiches and serve.

GRILLED CHICKEN SANDWICH

Serves 8

Chipotle Mayonnaise

1 can (7 oz/210 g) chipotle
    chilies in adobo sauce

4 cloves garlic

4 tsp (20 mL) firmly packed
    brown sugar

1 cup (250 mL) mayonnaise

½ cup (125 mL) sour cream

1 tbsp (15 mL) lemon juice

½ tsp (2 mL) kosher salt

Pesto Mayonnaise

1 cup (250 mL) mayonnaise

3 tbsp (15 mL) pesto

Grilled Chicken

1 cup (250 mL) lime juice

½ cup (125 mL) salad oil

¼ cup (60 mL) kosher salt

3 tbsp (45 mL) granulated garlic

2 tbsp (30 mL) dried oregano,
    crumbled

4 tsp (20 mL) pepper

1 tbsp (15 mL) chili powder

4 lb (1.8 kg) boneless
    chicken thighs

Sandwiches

Artisanal soft buns, halved
    horizontally

1 bunch fresh cilantro,
    tough stems discarded

For the chipotle mayonnaise, in a food processor, purée chilies. Set aside 3 tbsp (45 mL) chipotle purée. (Remaining purée can be frozen for another use.) Clean bowl of food processor and add garlic and brown sugar. Pulse to chop, scraping down sides of bowl. Add mayonnaise, sour cream, lemon juice, and salt; process to combine. Add 2 tbsp (30 mL) of the reserved chipotle purée; process to combine. Add more purée to taste. Refrigerate until needed. (Mayonnaise keeps, covered and refrigerated, for up to 3 weeks.)

For the pesto mayonnaise, stir together mayonnaise and pesto. Refrigerate until needed. (Mayonnaise keeps, covered and refrigerated, for up to 3 weeks.)

For the grilled chicken, in a large bowl, whisk together lime juice, oil, salt, granulated garlic, oregano, pepper, and chili powder. Add chicken thighs, turning to coat; marinate, covered and refrigerated, for 1 hour.

Preheat grill to high. Lift chicken out of marinade (discarding marinade). Grill, uncovered and turning frequently, until nicely browned, cooked through, and a meat thermometer reads 165°F (75°C).

For the sandwiches, spread chipotle mayonnaise on one cut side of each bun; spread pesto mayonnaise on the other side. Top with grilled chicken and cilantro (the more the better). Close sandwiches.

If you haven't heard of Maximus/Minimus, you don't live in Seattle. In the words of owner Kurt Dammeier, the truck is an "urban assault pig"—essentially a huge metal hog that rules the streets with amazing pulled pork (and chicken!) sandwiches.

Because the truck itself gets so much attention, we thought we would shine the spotlight on the chicken for a change. When you're making the chipotle mayo, you can do it extra-spicy for "maximus" or pull back on the chipotle for "minimus."

CHICKEN CUTLET SANDWICH

Serves 2

Pesto

1 cup (250 mL) olive oil

4 cloves garlic

2 cups (500 mL) packed fresh basil leaves

½ cup (125 mL) grated Parmigiano-Reggiano cheese

⅓ cup (75 mL) pine nuts, toasted

Kosher salt and pepper

Sandwiches

1 whole boneless, skinless chicken breast

2 eggs

½ cup (125 mL) grated Parmigiano-Reggiano cheese

1 cup (250 mL) olive oil (approx.)

1 cup (250 mL) dry Italian bread crumbs

2 ciabatta buns, halved horizontally

2 slices prosciutto

2 slices provolone cheese

1 ripe heirloom tomato, sliced

Handful of fresh baby arugula

½ tsp (2 mL) balsamic vinegar

Two contractors in South Carolina decided to hang up their tool belts and pursue another great Italian passion—feeding people. *Strada* means "street" and *cucina* means "kitchen," and this food truck couldn't have been more Italian. Using Grandma's old recipes, Brian, Jonathon, and sister Mia made this a family operation, offering up some of the best Italian cuisine on the scene. Make sure you find some fresh ciabatta buns for this delicious sandwich!

For the pesto, in a food processor combine ½ cup (125 mL) of the olive oil, garlic, basil, Parmesan, pine nuts, and salt and pepper to taste. Process until finely chopped. With motor running, drizzle in remaining oil to achieve desired consistency. Set aside.

For the sandwiches, using a sharp knife, cut chicken breast in half lengthwise. Butterfly chicken breast starting from the tenderloin (thick) side. Spread open on a cutting board. Cover chicken with plastic wrap. Using a mallet or heavy skillet, pound chicken until it is about ½ inch (1 cm) thick.

In a shallow dish large enough to hold the chicken, whisk together eggs, Parmesan, and a splash of the olive oil. Pour bread crumbs into a second shallow dish.

Heat ¼ inch (5 mm) oil in a large skillet over medium heat. When oil is hot, dip chicken in egg mixture, coating both sides; let excess egg drip off. Press chicken into bread crumbs, then flip to coat both sides. Fry chicken until golden and cooked through, about 4 minutes per side. Drain on paper towels. Drain most of oil from skillet.

Toast ciabatta buns. Meanwhile, heat skillet over medium-low heat. Return chicken to pan and top each piece with prosciutto and provolone. Cover and cook until cheese melts. Spread pesto on bottom half of each bun. Top with chicken, tomato slices, and arugula. Sprinkle with balsamic vinegar and close sandwiches.

THE ELLSWORTH

Serves 7 (with leftover biscuits)

Pickles

7 cups (1.75 L) water

½ cup (125 mL) salt

5 lb (2.25 kg) cucumbers

3¼ cups (810 mL) white vinegar

1¾ cups (425 mL) cider vinegar

½ cup (125 mL) dried pequin chilies

2 tbsp (30 mL) mustard seeds

12 cloves garlic

Chicken

1 egg

¾ cup (175 mL) buttermilk

1 tbsp (15 mL) Cajun spice

½ tsp (2 mL) cayenne pepper

7 small boneless, skin-on chicken breasts (each about 3 oz/85 g)

Canola oil for deep-frying

1 cup (250 mL) all-purpose flour

Salt and black pepper

Biscuits (makes 12)

2 cups (500 mL) all-purpose flour

½ cup (125 mL) cake-and-pastry flour

2 tbsp (30 mL) buttermilk powder

1 tbsp (15 mL) sugar

4 tsp (20 mL) baking powder

2 tsp (10 mL) salt

1¾ cups (425 mL) cold unsalted butter (3½ sticks), cut into small pieces

3 eggs

1¼ cups (300 mL) buttermilk

1 cup (250 mL) plain yogurt

Garnishes

Whole-grain Dijon mustard

Honey

At The Biscuit Bus in Denver, the motto is "Butter… it's not good for you but it's delicious." Husband-and-wife team Drew and Ashleigh Shader didn't originally plan on being in the food business, but today they're serving up the best biscuits and gravy we've come across.

Here's a great tip for making the biscuits: use *frozen* butter and *shred* it into the flour mixture like cheese. Trust me, it makes a world of difference!

Make the pickles 2 weeks ahead. In a large nonaluminum bowl, combine water and salt; stir until salt dissolves. Cut cucumbers into ¼-inch (5 mm) slices. Add cucumbers to brine and soak overnight.

Drain cucumbers and spread them in a single layer on a baking sheet lined with paper towels; allow to dry. In a large pot, combine white vinegar, cider vinegar, pequin chilies, mustard seeds, and garlic; bring to a boil. Add cucumbers; return to a boil and boil just until first pickle becomes translucent. Transfer cucumbers and liquid to a large non-aluminum bowl; refrigerate until cold. Cover and keep refrigerated for 2 weeks.

Marinate the chicken the day before. In a medium bowl, whisk together egg, buttermilk, Cajun spice, and cayenne. Add chicken, turning to coat. Marinate, covered and refrigerated, overnight.

For the biscuits, preheat oven to 375°F (190°C). Grease a baking sheet.

In the bowl of a stand mixer, sift together all-purpose flour, cake-and-pastry flour, buttermilk powder, sugar, baking powder, and salt. Add butter; cut in with a pastry blender or your fingertips until mixture resembles coarse crumbs. In a small bowl, whisk together eggs,

buttermilk, and yogurt. Fit mixer with dough hook. With mixer on lowest speed, slowly add buttermilk mixture to flour mixture; mix for 1½ minutes. The dough should be soft, but stir in a little more all-purpose flour if it is too wet.

Turn dough out onto a lightly floured work surface. Sprinkle dough with flour. Knead gently for 30 to 45 seconds. Roll out dough into a rectangle 1 inch (2.5 cm) thick. Fold into thirds; turn over dough. Roll out and fold 6 more times or until chips of butter are almost gone. Roll out dough until 1 inch (2.5 cm) thick. Cut out 12 biscuits using a 4-inch (10 cm) cookie cutter. Arrange biscuits on baking sheet. Bake for 18 minutes or until biscuits are light golden brown and a tester inserted horizontally comes out clean.

To finish the chicken, in a deep-fryer or deep, heavy saucepan, heat 2 inches (5 cm) of canola oil to 375°F (190°C). In a shallow dish, stir together flour with salt and pepper to taste. Dredge chicken in flour, coating thoroughly. Working in batches if necessary, fry chicken until golden and crispy, 12 to 15 minutes. Drain on paper towels.

Split biscuits horizontally. Put chicken on bottom halves; cover with mustard and honey to taste. Top with drained pickled cucumbers and finish with top of biscuit.

TURKEY MEATBALL SANDWICH

Serves 5 (with leftover marinara sauce)

Marinara Sauce

1 can (19 oz/540 mL) whole
   plum tomatoes
¼ cup (60 mL) coarsely
   chopped onion
¼ cup (60 mL) coarsely
   chopped carrots
¼ cup (60 mL) coarsely
   chopped celery
1½ tsp (7 mL) dried Italian
   herb seasoning
½ tsp (2 mL) sugar
½ tsp (2 mL) salt
½ tsp (2 mL) pepper
1 clove garlic
½ bay leaf

1½ cups (375 mL) red wine
½ tsp (2 mL) tomato paste
½ tsp (2 mL) chopped fresh basil

Turkey Meatballs

2 lb (900 g) ground turkey
1 egg, lightly beaten
½ cup (125 mL) panko bread crumbs
¼ cup (60 mL) grated
   Parmesan cheese
2 tbsp (30 mL) olive oil
1 tbsp (15 mL) dried Italian
   herb seasoning
1 tbsp (15 mL) finely chopped
   fresh basil
1 tbsp (15 mL) finely chopped
   green onions

1 tbsp (15 mL) minced garlic
1½ tsp (7 mL) fennel seeds
1 tsp (5 mL) onion powder
¼ tsp (1 mL) cayenne pepper
1 tsp (5 mL) salt
1 tsp (5 mL) black pepper

Sandwiches

5 hoagie buns, 8 inches (20 cm) long,
   halved horizontally
10 slices mozzarella cheese
2 tbsp (30 mL) chopped fresh basil
⅓ cup (75 mL) grated
   Parmesan cheese
5 pickled green peperoncini, sliced

For the marinara sauce, in a large saucepan, combine tomatoes, onion, carrots, celery, Italian seasoning, sugar, salt, pepper, garlic, bay leaf, and red wine. Bring to a boil, reduce heat, and simmer, uncovered and stirring occasionally, for 2 hours. Stir in tomato paste; simmer for 15 more minutes. Remove from heat and discard bay leaf. Stir in fresh basil. Using an immersion blender, blend until smooth. Keep warm.

For the meatballs, preheat oven to 475°F (240°C). In a large bowl, combine ground turkey, egg, panko crumbs, Parmesan, oil, Italian seasoning, basil, green onions, garlic, fennel seeds, onion powder, cayenne, salt, and black pepper. Mix well. Using a 2-tbsp (30 mL) scoop, make at least 20 meatballs; transfer to a large baking sheet. Bake for 10 minutes or until golden brown. Let cool.

For the sandwiches, preheat a griddle or large skillet over medium heat. Place hoagie buns cut sides up in pan. Top cut sides of bread with mozzarella. Toast until cheese is melted and bread is golden. Remove from pan. Place 4 meatballs in each hoagie; top with ¼ cup (60 mL) marinara sauce . Garnish with basil, Parmesan cheese, and peperoncini.

There are a few oddities that jump out at you when you first approach Le Truc. First of all, it's not even a truck, really. It's a converted school bus. Second, it is not just serving street food, it is serving intensely über-gourmet food that you just happen to eat on the street . . . or actually onboard the bus. In the words of owner Blake Tally, "It's not a food truck or a bus. It's a bus-taurant!"

TURKEY CAESAR SANDWICH

Serves 4

When patrons say that the only way to eat your sandwiches is to "unhinge your jaw like a cobra," you know you are making some big-ass sandwiches! At this popular Portland food truck, they don't ask, "Would you like fries with that?" You're getting them whether you want them or not, because lovebirds Brian and Lisa Wood serve the fries in their sandwiches—saving you time and money.

1 lb (450 g) turkey breast
Juice of 1 lemon
2 egg yolks
4 anchovy fillets
1½ tsp (7 mL) chopped garlic
1 tsp (5 mL) Dijon mustard
½ tsp (2 mL) Worcestershire sauce
Salt and pepper
⅓ cup (75 mL) extra-virgin olive oil
1 russet potato
Canola oil for deep-frying
8 slices bread
5 oz (140 g) Parmesan cheese, grated
18 leaves romaine lettuce

Preheat oven to 250°F (120°C). Slow-roast turkey breast in a small roasting pan until a meat thermometer reads 155°F (70°C), 3 to 4 hours. Cool in refrigerator. Thickly slice turkey crosswise.

Preheat grill to high. Grill turkey, uncovered, until grill marks appear, 3 to 4 minutes.

In a food processor, combine lemon juice, egg yolks, anchovies, garlic, mustard, Worcestershire sauce, and salt and pepper to taste; process just to mix. With motor running, drizzle in olive oil until emulsified. Adjust seasoning.

Cut unpeeled potato lengthwise into sticks ¼ inch (5 mm) thick. In a deep-fryer or deep, heavy saucepan, heat 2 inches (5 cm) of canola oil to 365°F (185°C). Fry potatoes for 5 to 7 minutes—do not let them color. Drain on paper towels and let cool. Heat oil to 365°F (185°C). Fry potatoes until golden brown and crispy, 2 to 3 minutes. Drain on paper towels.

Spread Caesar dressing on one side of each slice of bread. Sprinkle about 3 tbsp (45 mL) Parmesan over both sides of each sandwich. Arrange grilled turkey, lettuce, and fries on half of each sandwich. Sprinkle fries with remaining Parmesan and close sandwiches.

THANK YOU...
THANK YOU VERY MUCH

Serves 1

2 thick slices brioche bread

3 tbsp (45 mL) butter, at room temperature

¼ cup (60 mL) creamy peanut butter

1 banana, cut lengthwise in ¼-inch (5 mm) slices

3 slices applewood-smoked bacon, cooked until crisp

Honey

Generously butter one side of each slice of bread. Turn one slice butter side down; top with peanut butter, banana, and bacon. Drizzle with honey. Top with the second slice of bread, buttered side up.

Heat a nonstick griddle to medium heat (350°F/180°C). Cook sandwich on hot griddle until golden brown, 3 to 4 minutes per side. (Or grill in skillet over medium heat, turning once.)

People always ask me, "James, if Elvis ate at food trucks, what would he eat?" Actually no one has ever asked me that, but that is why we traveled to L.A., where we found the Pnut Butter Bar.

According to groovy PB princess Kharyn Deidre, the Thank You . . . Thank You Very Much was Elvis's favorite sandwich, one he would always ask for on the road. Not only that, it was apparently the last sandwich he ever had before his untimely demise.

BOURBON-MANGO PULLED PORK SANDWICH

Serves 20

Perfectly Spiced Slow Cooker Pork

2 bay leaves

1 boneless pork sirloin roast (4 lb/1.8 kg)

1 tsp (5 mL) salt

1 tsp (5 mL) garlic powder

1 tsp (5 mL) ground cumin

½ tsp (2 mL) crumbled dried oregano

½ tsp (2 mL) ground coriander

½ tsp (2 mL) cinnamon

2 cups (500 mL) water

Mango Jalapeño Slaw

1 medium green cabbage, shredded

2 ripe mangoes, peeled and diced

1 small red onion, thinly sliced and cut in 1-inch (2.5 cm) strips

2 jalapeño peppers, very thinly sliced

1 cup (250 mL) fresh cilantro, chopped

½ cup (125 mL) seasoned rice vinegar

½ cup (125 mL) lime juice

½ cup (125 mL) orange juice

Salt

Mango Barbecue Sauce

2 ripe mangoes

3 tbsp (45 mL) bourbon

2 tsp (10 mL) honey

1 tsp (5 mL) chipotle chili powder

3 cups (750 mL) barbecue sauce (not hickory flavor)

Sandwiches

Toasted sandwich buns or rolls

Tex-Mex: fusion resulting in the blending of American Texas cooking and Mexican cuisine. Tex-Med: food that you find in a crazy hot-pink food truck in the burbs of Austin, Texas.

Suburban mom Lisa "Lizzie" Allen served up classic Mediterranean recipes but added not-quite-classic ingredients like rooster sauce, cherry cola, and this mind-blowing pulled pork. What would Zorba the Greek say? I think Lizzie would have won him over.

For the slow cooker pork, place bay leaves in the bottom of a slow cooker. Put pork roast on top. Sprinkle pork evenly with salt, garlic powder, cumin, oregano, coriander, and cinnamon. Pour water around sides of pork, being careful not to rinse off spices. Cover and cook on low until pork shreds easily with a fork, 8 to 10 hours, turning meat once after 4 hours. (Meanwhile, make slaw and barbecue sauce.)

For the slaw, in a large bowl combine cabbage, mango, onion, jalapeño, cilantro, vinegar, lime juice, orange juice, and salt to taste. Toss gently. Marinate in the fridge for at least 1 hour. (Slaw keeps, refrigerated, for 2 days.)

For the mango barbecue sauce, peel and coarsely chop mangoes. In a large saucepan, use a potato masher to mash mangoes into a thick, chunky paste. Cook over medium-high heat until mango has reduced and darkened slightly, about 5 minutes. Stir in bourbon, honey, and chili powder. Bring to a simmer. Reduce heat to medium-low and simmer, stirring frequently, for 2 or 3 minutes, allowing alcohol in the bourbon to cook off. Stir in barbecue sauce. Remove from heat.

Transfer cooked pork to cutting board. Tent loosely with foil and let rest for 10 minutes. Shred meat with two forks, leaving some large chunks. Moisten meat as needed with cooking liquid.

Gently stir shredded pork into mango barbecue sauce, taking care not to break up the tender pork too much. Heat until warmed through.

Spoon pork onto toasted buns and top with slaw.

HUNTS POINT

AUTO SALES *And* SERVICE CENTER

AUTO GLASS

RIBS

NYS INSPECTION

NYS INSPECTION

NEW & USED TIRES

Computerized WHEEL ALIGNMENT

HEAT & AIR CONDITIONING ELECTRICAL *Repair*

Discount MUFFLER AND Custom EXHAUST SYSTEMS

ENGINE DIAGNOSTICS AND TUNE-UPS

BRAKES·SHOCKS STRUTS 718 991-8808

MOgridder's

MoGRIDDER'S WORLD FAMOUS SMOKED BBQ

BBQ FREE LOCAL DELIVERY 718 991-3046 www.MoGridder.com

BBQ RIBS & CHICKEN PULLED PORK

USED TIRE SALE

SMOKED PORK BUTT SANDWICH

Serves 4 (with lots of leftover pulled pork)

Mo Gridder's Dry Rub Barbecue Seasoning

2½ tbsp (37 mL) paprika

2 tbsp (30 mL) kosher salt

2 tbsp (30 mL) granulated sugar

1 tbsp (15 mL) raw or granulated brown sugar

1 tbsp (15 mL) chili powder

1 tbsp (15 mL) black pepper

1 tbsp (15 mL) onion powder

1 tsp (5 mL) cayenne pepper

1 tsp (5 mL) dried oregano

1 tsp (5 mL) dried thyme

Smoked Pork Butt

1 pork butt (4 lb/1.8 kg)

2 tbsp (30 mL) salt

2 tbsp (30 mL) granulated garlic or garlic powder

1 tbsp (15 mL) pepper

Mo Gridder's Barbecue Sauce

½ cup (125 mL) sugar

2 to 3 tsp (10 to 15 mL) freshly ground black pepper

2 tsp (10 mL) kosher salt

1 tsp (5 mL) granulated garlic or garlic powder

1 tsp (5 mL) ground oregano

½ tsp (2 mL) dried thyme

½ cup (125 mL) white vinegar (approx.)

1 cup (250 mL) molasses

1 cup (250 mL) ketchup

¾ cup (175 mL) prepared mustard

1 tsp (5 mL) cayenne pepper (optional)

Sandwiches

4 buns, halved horizontally and toasted

For the dry rub seasoning, in a small bowl, stir together paprika, salt, granulated sugar, brown sugar, chili powder, pepper, onion powder, cayenne, oregano, and thyme. (Dry rub keeps, in an airtight container, for up to 6 months.)

For the smoked pork, season pork all over in this order: salt, granulated garlic, pepper, and all the dry rub seasoning.

Prepare grill or smoker with wood chips of your choice; preheat grill on high until chips smoke vigorously, about 20 minutes. Lower heat to medium. Place pork on greased grill over drip pan. Close lid and smoke pork at 225°F (110°C), adding more wood chips if necessary, for 10½ hours or until fork-tender. (Meanwhile, make barbecue sauce.)

For the barbecue sauce, in a medium nonaluminum saucepan, combine sugar, black pepper, salt, granulated garlic, oregano, and thyme. Stir in enough vinegar to make a loose paste. In a small bowl, stir together molasses, ketchup, mustard, and cayenne (if using). Stir into spice paste. Bring to a boil, stirring constantly. Reduce heat and simmer, stirring occasionally, until thick, about 20 minutes.

Transfer cooked meat to a cutting board; chop meat. Serve meat on buns with barbecue sauce.

Only in America can you get an oil change and a pulled pork sandwich at the *same* place for $34.95. What started out as owner Fred Donnelly's plan to give his auto customers a bite to eat while they waited for repairs has turned into the coolest barbecue trailer in the nation. Everything is smoked nice and long, and you can *taste* the time and love that go into every menu item.

PORCHETTA SANDWICH

Serves 12

Onion Marmalade

7 onions, sliced

4 tsp (20 mL) olive oil

2 tbsp (30 mL) salt

1 tbsp (15 mL) fennel seeds

¾ cup (175 mL) balsamic vinegar

Porchetta

1 tbsp (15 mL) lemon zest

1½ tsp (7 mL) lemon juice

1 tbsp (15 mL) chopped fresh rosemary

1 tbsp (15 mL) chopped fresh sage

1½ tsp (7 mL) chopped fresh marjoram

2 tbsp (30 mL) fennel seeds, toasted and lightly crushed

1 tbsp (15 mL) minced garlic

4 bay leaves, toasted and ground

1 tbsp (15 mL) kosher salt

1 tbsp (15 mL) black pepper

1½ tsp (7 mL) light pinot grigio

1 boneless center-cut pork loin, with belly and skin (4 lb/1.8 kg)

Sandwiches

12 ciabatta buns, halved horizontally

Fresh micro greens such as curly cress

Thomas Odermatt has it the best possible way: he owns the first and the best (his own words) rolling rotisserie on the road. In his opinion, rotisserie cooking is the best and only self-basting way to cook meat. Judging by the crowds that follow him all over San Francisco, this guy knows something other food trucks do not.

Where an average food truck is lucky to serve a hundred tickets in a lunch, the day we were there to shoot, Thomas and his crew dished out 480 helpings of porchetta, chicken, and delicious juice-drenched potatoes.

For the onion marmalade, in a large saucepan over medium-high heat, combine onions and olive oil. Cook, stirring occasionally, until onions look a bit dry and begin to turn golden brown. Stir in salt and fennel. Reduce heat to very low and stir in balsamic vinegar, a few splashes at a time. Continue cooking, stirring occasionally, for 6 to 7 hours or until onions taste sweet—the longer, the lower, the better. Let cool. (Marmalade keeps, covered and refrigerated, for 2 weeks.)

For the porchetta, in a small bowl, stir together lemon zest, lemon juice, rosemary, sage, marjoram, fennel seeds, garlic, bay leaves, salt, pepper, and wine.

If pork is overly fatty, trim excess fat. Lay pork skin side down. Cut horizontally into pork belly above the skin, making pockets, making sure you do not cut into the meat. Push one-third of porchetta spice into pockets in pork belly; spread remaining porchetta spice evenly over pork. Roll up belly around loin, sealing it with skin flap. Tie roast tightly with kitchen string every 2 inches (5 cm). (Refrigerate, covered, overnight for best flavor.)

Preheat oven to 450°F (230°C). Place roast on a rack in a roasting pan, seam side up. Roast for 30 minutes. Lower oven temperature to 350°F (180°C) and continue to roast, basting if desired, for another 1¼ hours, or until a meat thermometer reads 130°F (55°C). During the last 5 minutes, broil roast, turning frequently, until skin is crisp and golden brown. Let porchetta rest for 15 minutes before serving.

Remove string and cut porchetta into ½-inch (1 cm) slices. Put porchetta slices inside buns. Top with a thin layer of onion marmalade and a handful of micro greens.

PHILLY CHEESE STEAK

Serves 4

6 tbsp (90 mL) vegetable oil

1 large onion, sliced

1 sweet green pepper, sliced

1 sweet red pepper, sliced

Salt and black pepper

1½ lb (675 g) rib-eye steak,
  thinly sliced

Steak seasoning (optional)

4 crusty Italian rolls, halved
  horizontally

White American cheese or
  processed cheese spread

Heat a large skillet over medium heat. Add 3 tbsp (45 mL) oil. Add onion and peppers; fry until softened and starting to color. Season with salt and black pepper. Remove from pan.

Add remaining oil to pan; increase heat to medium-high. Season steak with steak seasoning (if using) or salt and black pepper; sauté steak quickly on both sides. Remove from pan.

Stuff each roll with steak. Top with onions and peppers. Top with cheese.

Where did we find one of the best Philly cheese steak sandwiches in America? Philly? New York? Pittsburgh? Nope. In a gun store parking lot in Las Vegas. I'm not kidding! This is the kind of thing that happens on *Eat St.* Every time we think we've seen it all, the next food truck comes along.

Owner Andrew Barbieri wasn't a trained chef, but his friends went so crazy over his hot sandwiches that he opened up a truck and never looked back. I guarantee that this classic cheese steak sandwich will hit the spot.

BACON-WRAPPED PORK MEATLOAF SANDWICH

Serves 10 to 12

When Chef Matt Gennuso makes hotdogs, he goes whole hog! When making his gourmet sausages, he uses meat from his commissary restaurant Chez Pascal, where he practices "whole animal butchery." On our show we try to stay away from foods that you'd expect from a food truck, so to get on our radar you *have* to be cranking out some good dogs. Pork, duck, and rabbit are just some of the meats that Matt blends into the wieners at Hewtin's Dogs in Providence, Rhode Island.

And if there isn't enough pork in these dogs for you, then he'll wrap pork in bacon and call it a sandwich!

Meatloaf

2 tbsp (30 mL) bacon fat

¾ cup (175 mL) minced onion

1 tbsp (15 mL) minced garlic

1 tbsp (15 mL) chopped fresh flat-leaf parsley

1 tbsp (15 mL) chopped fresh sage

5 oz (140 g) sliced bacon

3 eggs

3 lb (1.5 kg) ground pork shoulder

2½ cups (625 mL) dry bread crumbs

1⅓ cups (325) grated Parmesan cheese

1 tbsp (15 mL) kosher salt

1 tsp (2 mL) pepper

Sandwiches

10 to 12 soft burger buns

Coleslaw

Spicy fig compote or other topping

Make the meatloaf the day before. In a medium saucepan over medium heat, melt bacon fat. Add onions; cover and cook until translucent. Stir in garlic; cook for 2 more minutes. Stir in parsley and sage; cook, stirring frequently, for another minute. Transfer mixture to a bowl and refrigerate until cool.

Preheat oven to 350°F (180°C). Line bottom and sides of a 9- × 5-inch (2 L) loaf pan with bacon slices, arranging them parallel to the short end and slightly overlapping, with their ends hanging over the edges.

In a large bowl, beat eggs. Add ground pork, bread crumbs, Parmesan, salt, pepper, and onion mixture. Mix just until thoroughly combined. Add meat mixture to lined pan, filling three-quarters of the way to the top; pat it down to make it smooth and even. Fold overhanging ends of bacon up and over meat mixture to cover it completely.

Place loaf pan inside a larger, deeper pan; add boiling water to come halfway up sides of loaf pan. Bake for 1½ hours or until a meat thermometer reads 150°F (65°C). Remove loaf pan from water bath and refrigerate meatloaf until fully cooled. (It's best if it sits overnight.)

For the sandwiches, lightly oil a large nonstick skillet and heat over medium heat. Turn meatloaf out of pan; thickly slice meatloaf. Add meatloaf to skillet and brown both sides. Meanwhile, toast buns.

Spread coleslaw on bottom half of each bun, add a meatloaf slice, and dress with desired topping.

TACOS, WRAPS
& CONES

Now we're getting down to it. The kind of street food that separates the real foodies from the hipsters and wannabes. *Everyone* has had their share of fries, hotdogs, and burgers, but it's time to get our fusion on and get ethnic. We're going to Hawaii for pork tacos, Vancouver for Malaysian burritos, and Philadelphia for a French crêpe that would put any Jewish deli to shame.

After all, we really couldn't say that we searched out "the most daring and delicious street food around" until we found the best Mexican burrito in London, England. Get your flavor passport out, because this is going to be a trip!

TACOS, WRAPS & CONES

RAJAS CON QUESO

Serves 8

Street food and public transportation have always gone hand in hand, but this Tampa taco maestro is driving it to a whole new level. From his humble beginnings at his tiny taco stand, to his twenty-four-hour roadside bus, Rene Valenzuela is now cranking out thousands of tacos a day. Authentic Mexican tacos are getting harder and harder to find with so much fusion going on in the street scene, but Rene uses recipes straight from his Mayan ancestors.

Rene stresses that you *have* to expose the poblanos to open flame—it's the only way to bring out the natural taste and will get *you* on his flavor bus!

5 poblano chilies
1 jalapeño pepper (optional)
1 cup (250 mL) queso fresco cheese
1 tbsp (15 mL) corn oil
¼ cup (60 mL) finely chopped onion
½ cup (125 mL) diced tomato
½ cup (125 mL) corn kernels (preferably cooked on cob and then cut off)
1 cup (250 mL) sour cream
Salt
8 small tostadas or warmed corn tortillas

On a grill or gas stove and using metal tongs, put poblano chilies and jalapeño (if using) over an open flame to burn the skins, turning peppers to evenly char. When all the skin is black, seal poblanos in a plastic bag (the steam will help release the skins). With the help of a napkin, pull skin away. Do not rinse. Cut stems away, remove seeds, and cut poblanos into strips. Set aside. If using a jalapeño, remove stem but do not peel or seed; finely dice, and set aside. Cut queso fresco into strips like french fries.

In a large skillet, heat oil over medium-high heat. Fry onion until translucent. Add tomato; fry until softened. Add corn; cook for 1 minute. Stir in sour cream and queso fresco. Turn heat down to medium and warm the mixture (don't let it boil or the cream might curdle). Stir in poblanos and jalapeño (if using). Warm for 1 minute. If poblanos are too crunchy or raw, cook for few minutes longer until soft. Add salt to taste.

Serve on crunchy tostadas or in warm corn tortillas as tacos.

TUNA TATAKI TACOS

Serves 2

Ponzu Sauce

½ cup (125 mL) chicken stock

½ cup (125 mL) soy sauce

¼ cup (60 mL) bonito flakes

¼ cup (60 mL) rice wine vinegar

¼ cup (60 mL) sweet rice wine

¼ cup (60 mL) lime juice

1 tbsp (15 mL) minced garlic

1 tbsp (15 mL) hot pepper flakes

1 tbsp (15 mL) black pepper

¼ cup (60 mL) cornstarch

¼ cup (60 mL) water

Seaweed Salad

¼ cup (60 mL) wakame seaweed

½ sweet yellow pepper, julienned

¼ cup (60 mL) julienned cucumber

Tuna

2 tbsp (30 mL) cooking oil

1 tuna steak

Salt and pepper

Fried Wontons

1 cup (250 mL) cooking oil

1 wonton wrapper, cut in strips

Tacos

2 small flour tortillas

For the ponzu, in a medium saucepan, whisk together chicken stock, soy sauce, bonito flakes, rice wine vinegar, sweet rice wine, lime juice, garlic, pepper flakes, and black pepper. Bring to a boil. Meanwhile, stir together cornstarch and water. Once sauce has come to a boil, pour in about ¼ cup (60 mL) of the cornstarch mixture. Stir ponzu and return to a boil. Stir in more cornstarch mixture if needed (ponzu should be thick enough to glaze the tuna without running off). Remove from heat and set aside.

For the seaweed salad, soak wakame in water until it fully expands. Drain well. In a medium bowl, toss together wakame, yellow pepper, and cucumber. Set aside.

For the tuna, heat oil in a skillet over medium-high heat. Sprinkle both sides of tuna steak with salt and pepper. Sear tuna for 15 to 30 seconds per side. Transfer tuna to a cutting board and cover loosely with foil to keep warm.

For the fried wontons, heat oil in a large saucepan over medium-high heat. Fry wonton strips until golden brown. Drain on paper towels.

To finish the tacos, thinly slice tuna steak. In a nonstick skillet over medium heat, heat tortillas on each side until hot but still pliable. Divide sliced tuna between hot tortillas. Top with seaweed salad. Glaze tuna and seaweed salad with ponzu. Top with fried wontons.

"Going local" is easy when your local meats are chicken and beef, but what do you do when your truck is in Baton Rouge, Louisiana? Local meats like catfish are easy to come by, but what about "the other white meat" in the South—alligator? One food truck has risen to the challenge and includes the large lizard on its menu.

We're assuming that getting fresh alligator in your neck of the woods might not be possible, but this tuna taco still has some serious bite to it!

MAHI MAHI FISH TACOS

Serves 2

When Ingrid and Yayo Jiménez opened their food truck in Nashville, they thought it was cool that they abbreviated the words "Original Mexican Grill" in its name, but their food is so good that people are saying OMG for other reasons! This family operation brings authentic gourmet Mexican to Music City, and locals are flocking and rocking to get their hands on Yayo's latest hit.

In our opinion his *greatest* hit is the Mahi Mahi Fish Taco. There is nothing B-side about this creation; it is right off the streets of Mexico, but with a bit of a twist. The top-secret cilantro sauce is a secret no more, so now you can make your own hit.

Coleslaw

1½ cups (375 mL) shredded red cabbage
1½ cups (375 mL) shredded green cabbage
1½ cups (375 mL) shredded carrots
2½ cups 625 mL) orange juice
Salt and pepper

Cilantro Sauce

2½ cups (625 mL) sour cream
1½ cups (375 mL) chopped fresh cilantro
½ cup (125 mL) lemon juice
4 large cloves garlic, mashed to a paste
Salt and pepper

Fish

2 lb (900 g) mahi mahi fillets
3 cups (750 mL) dark beer
1 cup (250 mL) canola oil
4 cups (1 L) all-purpose flour
4 tsp (20 mL) cayenne pepper
4 tsp (20 mL) paprika
2 tsp (10 mL) salt

Tacos

8 small corn tortillas

For the coleslaw, in a large bowl, toss together red cabbage, green cabbage, and carrots. Add orange juice and salt and pepper to taste. Toss again. Set aside.

For the cilantro sauce, in a small bowl, stir together sour cream, cilantro, lemon juice, garlic, and salt and pepper to taste. Set aside.

For the fish, cut fillets crosswise into even strips. Marinate in beer for about 5 minutes. Meanwhile, heat oil in a large skillet over medium heat. In a shallow dish, combine flour, cayenne, paprika, and salt.

Dredge fish strips in seasoned flour. Working in batches if necessary, fry strips in hot oil until golden brown, 90 seconds to 2 minutes. Drain on paper towels.

To finish the tacos, in a separate skillet, heat tortillas over medium heat until warm but still pliable. Using 2 tortillas per taco, fill with most of the coleslaw, top with mahi mahi strips, add some more coleslaw on top, and finish with cilantro sauce.

DRUNKEN SHRIMP TACOS

Serves 2

To own a food truck you have to have passion, but we found a chef who drives twenty-five miles out of his way every day to find just the right bread for his shrimpy creations with huge taste. In Santa Monica, married couple Chandra and Neil Macleod are constantly arguing over who the real pimp daddy is, but either way, their truck, the Shrimp Pimp, has an army of loyal fans who swear it's the best food truck in town.

As Neil says, "Shrimpin' ain't easy but it sure is fun." And fun is exactly what you will have with this dish. After all, there are shrimp and then there are *drunken* shrimp. Sherry mixed with rice vinegar gives it kick. Pimp-pimp, hooray!

Topping

1 cup (250 mL) orange juice
½ cup (125 mL) lime juice
¼ cup (60 mL) rice vinegar
2 tbsp (30 mL) sugar
1 jalapeño pepper, seeded and julienned
1 cup (250 mL) julienned daikon radish
1 cup (250 mL) julienned carrot

Drunken Shrimp

1 lb (450 g) large shrimp, peeled and deveined
¼ cup (60 mL) chopped green onions

1 tsp (5 mL) grated fresh ginger
1 clove garlic, minced
1 tsp (5 mL) sugar
3 tbsp (45 mL) soy sauce
2 tbsp (30 mL) water
2 tbsp (30 mL) corn oil
2 tbsp (30 mL) dry sherry
1 tbsp (15 mL) rice vinegar
2 tbsp (30 mL) cornstarch

Tacos

4 small corn tortillas
Fresh cilantro sprigs and orange slices for garnish

For the topping, in a medium bowl, combine orange juice, lime juice, vinegar, and sugar, stirring to dissolve sugar. Set aside.

Bring a pot of water to a boil. Add jalapeño, daikon, and carrot. Boil for 2 minutes. Transfer vegetables to a bowl of ice water to stop the cooking. Drain well. Transfer to juice mixture; toss gently to coat thoroughly.

For the drunken shrimp, rinse shrimp in cold water; pat dry. In a large skillet, combine green onions, ginger, garlic, sugar, soy sauce, water, oil, sherry, and rice vinegar. Stir over medium heat until marinade starts to bubble. Whisk in cornstarch a little at a time until sauce is thickened. Add shrimp to sauce and cook, turning, for 3 to 4 minutes or until just cooked through.

To finish tacos, cover tortillas with a damp towel; microwave on High for 15 to 20 seconds. Divide shrimp mixture among tortillas. Spoon topping over shrimp. Garnish with cilantro and a couple of orange segments.

PRAWNS N' ROSES

Serves 4

1 box (1 lb/454 g) kataifi
(shredded phyllo pastry)

1 egg

¼ cup (60 mL) all-purpose flour

1 lb (450 g) extra-large shrimp,
deveined and tails removed

2 cups (500 mL) grapeseed oil

Salt and pepper

4 small flour or corn tortillas

½ cup (125 mL) shredded
green cabbage

1 jalapeño pepper, thinly sliced

1 bunch green onions, thinly sliced

On a plate, separate kataifi into 4-inch (10 cm) strands. In a shallow dish, beat egg. In another shallow dish, combine flour with salt and pepper to taste. Dip each shrimp in flour, then in egg, letting excess drip off. Roll in kataifi, coating thoroughly.

Heat oil in a large saucepan over medium-high heat. When oil is hot, and working in batches if necessary, carefully add shrimp; fry for 2 to 3 minutes, until light golden brown on both sides. Drain on paper towels.

In a skillet over medium heat, warm tortillas, one at a time, until warm but still pliable.

Place 4 or 5 shrimp on each tortilla. Top with cabbage, jalapeño, and green onions.

To say that truck owner Shellie Kitchen (yep, that's her name) is scrappy would be an understatement. She is an adorable fireball and she loves to cook! She started the Brass Knuckle truck in San Francisco because she wanted to take common sandwiches and tacos, punch them up, and kick them to the curb. She may be tiny, but to hear her describe her recipes with such passion, let's just say that I wouldn't want to get in her way.

Kitchen takes the common shrimp taco and karate-chops your senses. I've had my share of shrimp dishes on our show, but in this one, the texture of the fried kataifi is out of this world.

CHICKEN FRESCA TACOS

Serves 8

Tequila-Lime Marinated Chicken

Zest of 1 lime

Juice of 5 limes

Juice of 2 oranges

¼ cup (60 mL) gold tequila

1 tbsp (15 mL) honey

1 large jalapeño pepper, seeded and minced

5 cloves garlic, minced

½ bunch fresh cilantro, chopped

2 tbsp (30 mL) kosher salt

1 tbsp (15 mL) guajillo chili powder

2 tsp (10 mL) black pepper

1½ lb (675 g) boneless, skinless chicken breasts, diced

Pico de Gallo

4 Roma tomatoes, diced

½ red onion, finely chopped

Juice of 1 lime

2 cloves garlic, minced

1 jalapeño pepper, seeded and finely chopped

1 tsp (5 mL) kosher salt

Freshly ground black pepper

Tacos

1 tbsp (15 mL) vegetable oil

8 small flour or corn tortillas

10 oz (280 g) white American cheese, shredded

2 tbsp (30 mL) chopped fresh cilantro

For the marinated chicken, in a medium bowl, combine lime zest, lime juice, orange juice, tequila, and honey. Add jalapeño, garlic, cilantro, salt, chili powder, and black pepper. Whisk thoroughly until chili powder and salt are dissolved. Add chicken, turning to coat well. Marinate, covered and refrigerated, for 3 to 4 hours.

For the pico de gallo, in a nonaluminum bowl, toss together tomatoes, onion, and lime juice. Add garlic, jalapeño, salt, and pepper to taste. Stir well. Refrigerate for 1 hour.

To finish the tacos, heat oil in a large skillet over high heat. Remove chicken from marinade (reserving marinade); sear chicken on all sides, about 20 seconds. Pour marinade over chicken and continuously turn chicken until cooked through.

Meanwhile, heat tortillas in a large skillet over medium heat until warm but still pliable.

Spoon chicken over tortillas. Top with pico de gallo and sprinkle with cheese. Serve garnished with cilantro.

When you realize that Mac and Harrison at Atlanta's Tex's Tacos combine chicken *and* tequila in a taco, you understand why their lineups are so crazy long! It is definitely the reason their Chicken Fresco Taco is one of the top sellers—there are other ingredients too, just not as fun.

These two college friends wanted to bring Tex-Mex (or Texican) fusion to Georgia, and many of their fans say they nailed it right on the head. Using fresh, local ingredients helps too. They are important, but let's face it, still not as exciting as the tequila.

THAI PORK TACOS

Serves 10

Aloha! If you're on the island of Oahu and you know Camille, then you probably know about her wheels. And if you know about her wheels, then you've had some of the most delicious tacos being served out of a truck *anywhere*!

Most chefs have access to local ingredients, but when you're a chef in Kailua, your ingredients grow on the trees right next to your truck! How local is that? And no one is combining these local flavors quite like Camille Komine. In addition to her super skill as a chef, her fans tell us she has everything it takes to run a great food truck: a smile, a big personality, and a great sense of humor.

Pork
2 lb (900 g) pork shoulder or butt
1 can (14 oz/400 mL) coconut milk
1 cup (250 mL) water
3 tbsp (45 mL) Thai red chili paste
1 tbsp (15 mL) grated fresh ginger
2 tsp (10 mL) salt
6 cloves garlic, peeled
8 kaffir lime leaves
4 stalks lemongrass (light part only), cut in 1-inch (2.5 cm) pieces

Pico de Gallo
4 tomatoes, finely chopped
1 onion, finely chopped
4 to 6 jalapeños, minced

Slaw
1 cup (250 mL) mayonnaise
1 tbsp (15 mL) mirin
1 tbsp (15 mL) agave syrup
6 cups (1.5 L) shredded green cabbage

Tacos
6 small corn tortillas
Chopped fresh cilantro

For the pork, preheat oven to 300°F (150°C). Place pork in large Dutch oven. In a bowl, whisk together coconut milk, water, chili paste, ginger, and salt. Add garlic, lime leaves, and lemongrass. Pour mixture over pork and cover tightly with lid. Bake for 4 hours or until pork is fork-tender. Transfer pork to a cutting board; let rest for 15 minutes. Shred pork.

For the pico de gallo, in a bowl, combine tomatoes, onion, and jalapeños. Stir well. Set aside.

Just before serving, make the slaw. In a large bowl, whisk together mayonnaise, mirin, and agave syrup. Add cabbage; toss to coat well.

To finish the tacos, warm tortillas in a skillet over medium heat until warm but still pliable. Place about 3 tbsp (45 mL) shredded pork on each tortilla. Top with slaw, pico de gallo, and cilantro.

CHIPOTLE CHUCK STEAK BURRITOS WITH HABANERO HOT SAUCE

Serves 6

Finding good Mexican food in the streets of London is as easy as finding a Scotch egg in Tijuana—that is to say, near impossible.

Simon Luard didn't think his last name sounded Mexican enough, so he added an o, and tickety-boo, guv'nor, the best burrito truck in London was born. Simon cooks his chuck steak for a good two hours in his special spicy brine before even *thinking* of combining it with the other ingredients and rolling it into the magic of the tortilla. Your friends will be lining up—sorry, queuing up—to try this one!

Luardos Chipotle Chuck Steak

1 tbsp (15 mL) olive oil

1 onion, thinly sliced

1 heaping tsp (7 mL) hot smoked paprika

1 heaping tsp (7 mL) ground cumin

½ tsp (2 mL) cinnamon (or 1 cinnamon stick)

1 lb (450 g) chuck steak, cut in 1-inch (2.5 cm) cubes

2 tbsp (30 mL) dried oregano

1 cup (250 mL) chipotle chilies in adobo sauce, chopped

1 cup (250 mL) water

Salt and pepper

2 oz (55 g) dark chocolate, chopped

Habanero Hot Sauce

6 habanero peppers

Juice of ½ lime

Pinch of sugar

3 tbsp (45 mL) olive oil

Tomato Salsa

4 ripe tomatoes, finely diced

½ Spanish onion, finely chopped

½ red onion, finely chopped

1 bird's eye chili (optional), minced

Handful of chopped fresh cilantro

2 pinches of sugar

Pinch of sea salt

Juice of 1 lime

Olive oil

Guacamole

4 Hass avocados

Juice of 1 lime

Olive oil

½ clove garlic, crushed

¼ jalapeño pepper, finely chopped

6 sprigs fresh cilantro, coarsely chopped

½ red onion, finely chopped

½ tomato, finely chopped

Salt and black pepper

Burritos

6 large flour tortillas

1 cup (250 mL) shredded Monterey Jack cheese

2 cups (500 mL) long-grain rice, cooked until fluffy (not wet)

1 can (19 oz/540 mL) black beans, drained and rinsed

Coarsely chopped fresh cilantro

Shredded iceberg lettuce

Sour cream

For the chipotle chuck steak, heat oil in a large saucepan over medium heat. Fry onion, stirring frequently, until soft. Stir in paprika, cumin, and cinnamon; fry for another minute. Add chuck steak, oregano, chipotles, water, and salt and pepper to taste. Give the whole thing a good stir. Bring to a boil, reduce heat, cover, and simmer for 2 hours or until meat can be easily flaked with a fork, adding more water if necessary. Add chocolate and stir until melted. (Meanwhile, make habanero hot sauce and salsa.) Remove cinnamon stick (if using).

For the habanero hot sauce, in a blender or food processor, combine habanero peppers, lime juice, sugar, and oil. Process until smooth. Set aside.

For the salsa, in a medium bowl, combine tomatoes, Spanish onion, red onion, chili (if using), cilantro, sugar, salt, lime juice, and a drizzle of olive oil. Stir well. Taste and add a little more lime juice or sugar if required. Set aside.

Shortly before serving, make the guacamole. Scoop avocado flesh into a medium bowl; roughly mash with a fork. Add lime juice, a good drizzle of olive oil, garlic, jalapeño, cilantro, onion, tomato, and salt and black pepper to taste. Stir well.

To finish the burritos, one at a time, toast tortillas in a large skillet over medium heat until slightly brown but still pliable. Sprinkle with cheese partway through heating so cheese starts to melt. Transfer burrito to a work surface and top with rice, black beans, chuck steak, cilantro, guacamole, habanero hot sauce, tomato salsa, lettuce, and sour cream, using as much or as little as you prefer. Fold up bottom, then fold in sides.

THE SLOPPY JO

Serves 10

Pickled Onions

Juice of 2½ large oranges

Juice of 2 limes

1½ tsp (7 mL) salt

½ tsp (2 mL) sugar

½ jalapeño pepper, seeded and diced

2½ onions, sliced

Red Chili Sauce

¾ cup (175 mL) New Mexico
    red chili powder

1 tbsp (15 mL) garlic salt

½ tsp (2 mL) ground cumin

3 cups (750 mL) water

¾ cup (175 mL) strained orange juice

1 tbsp (15 mL) canola oil

Sloppy Jos

5 lb (2.3 kg) boneless pork shoulder

10 eggs

10 large flour tortillas, warmed

With some food trucks you know exactly what you're getting into when you hear their name. We went down to Las Vegas to check out Jolene Mannina's truck, Sloppi Jo's, and her spin on New Mexican, and let's just say I wouldn't wear your Sunday best when trying her food.

Sloppi Jo's signature sandwich is probably something you've had many times before, but not the way Mannina does it. Get ready for some kick from that red chili sauce!

For the pickled onions, in a bowl stir together orange juice, lime juice, salt, sugar, and jalapeño. In a pot of boiling water, blanch onions for 15 seconds. Drain, then immediately add to juice mixture. Let sit at room temperature for at least 2 hours.

For the red chili sauce, in a large saucepan, combine chili powder, garlic salt, cumin, water, orange juice, and oil. Simmer over low heat for 25 minutes or until desired consistency.

For the Sloppy Jo, preheat oven to 350°F (180°C). Trim excess fat from pork and cut meat into ½-inch (1 cm) cubes. Spread pork in a roasting pan. Sprinkle with salt; toss to coat well. Pour red chili sauce over pork; cover pan tightly with foil. Roast for 3 hours. Remove foil and roast for another 30 minutes. The pork will be very tender and easy to pull apart when done. Pull pork apart if desired.

For each serving, in a bowl, combine pork and an egg; toss. Spoon filling onto warmed tortilla; top with pickled onions. Fold up bottom, then fold in sides.

MALAYSIAN LIME-CHILI TOFU GRILLED BURRITOS

Serves 6

Roaming Dragon in Vancouver was one of the first trucks we featured on *Eat St.* Many, many trucks and chefs later, it is still one of the best, and you're going to understand why with this recipe. I still remember the first time I tried Don Letendre's incredible fusion cuisine. I knew instantly that this truck was going to be a huge hit. The six basic items on the menu contain over four hundred ingredients and combine the best old-world Asian techniques with a new-world Grumman '67 truck.

These burritos may *sound* intimidating, but you can do it. It just takes a little Zen-like patience... and some shredded sui choy cabbage.

Pickled Red Cabbage

½ red onion, thinly sliced

1 cup (250 mL) thinly shredded red cabbage

½ cup (125 mL) packed brown sugar

¼ cup (60 mL) cider or malt vinegar

Malaysian Peanut Sauce

1 cup (250 mL) garlic cloves

1 cup (250 mL) chopped galangal

15 kaffir lime leaves

½ cup (125 mL) vegetable oil

5 cups (1.25 L) skinless roasted unsalted peanuts, coarsely chopped

2 cups (500 mL) shaved palm sugar

2 cups (500 mL) kecap manis (sweet soy sauce), plus extra for drizzling

¼ cup (60 mL) sambal badjak

Carrot Salad

3 tbsp (45 mL) rice vinegar

1 tbsp (15 mL) mirin

2 tbsp (30 mL) sugar

2 tbsp (30 mL) sesame oil

1 large carrot, shaved into long ribbons

¼ cucumber, halved lengthwise and sliced

2 to 3 tbsp (30 to 45 mL) coarsely chopped fresh cilantro

½ cup (125 mL) unsalted peanut halves

Burritos

3 tbsp (45 mL) canola oil

1 lb (450 g) firm tofu, cut in ½- × 1-inch pieces

3 cups (750 mL) shredded sui choy (napa) cabbage

¾ cup (175 mL) shredded red cabbage

6 large flour tortillas

½ lb (225 g) spinach leaves

¾ cup (175 mL) julienned carrots (about 2 medium carrots)

Make the pickled red cabbage a day or so ahead. In a large nonreactive bowl, combine onion, cabbage, sugar, and vinegar; stir to combine. Cover and chill for 24 hours, stirring occasionally. (Pickled cabbage keeps, refrigerated, for up to 3 days.)

For the peanut sauce, in a blender combine garlic, galangal, lime leaves, and ¼ cup (60 mL) of the oil. Process until very finely chopped. Heat remaining ¼ cup (60 mL) oil in a large, deep skillet over very low heat. Add garlic mixture; cook gently, stirring frequently, until garlic is cooked

but not coloring. Add peanuts, palm sugar, kecap manis, and sambal badjak; stir well. Add enough water to cover peanut mixture. Cook, stirring constantly (peanuts burn easily), until sauce thickens, about 45 minutes. Let cool.

For the carrot salad, in a small bowl, combine vinegar, mirin, sugar, and sesame oil; whisk until sugar is dissolved. In a medium bowl, combine carrot ribbons, cucumber, cilantro, and peanuts. Toss with vinaigrette to taste. Set aside.

For the burritos, in a large skillet, heat 2 tbsp (30 mL) of the oil over medium-high heat. Fry tofu until golden and crispy on all sides, about 5 minutes per side. Drain on paper towels. Wipe out skillet.

Divide sui choy cabbage and red cabbage among flour tortillas. Top each serving with ¾ cup (175 mL) peanut sauce. Arrange tofu over sauce; top with pickled red cabbage, spinach, and julienned carrots. Fold in bottom and top, then fold in sides.

Heat remaining 1 tbsp (15 mL) oil in skillet over medium heat. Cook burritos, starting seam side down, until golden brown on both sides. Cut each burrito in half on the diagonal with a serrated knife. Drizzle with kecap manis. Serve with carrot salad.

SMOKED SALMON CRÊPES

Serves 6 to 8

Crêpe Batter

2 large eggs

1 cup (250 mL) milk

⅓ cup (75 mL) water

1 cup (250 mL) all-purpose flour

¼ tsp (1 mL) salt

2 tbsp (30 mL) butter, melted, plus extra for coating pan

Filling

2½ cups (625 mL) cream cheese, softened

3 tbsp (45 mL) mayonnaise

¼ to ⅓ lb (115 to 170 g) smoked salmon

12 to 16 thick slices tomato

Thinly sliced red onion

Sliced roasted red peppers

Sliced sweet green peppers

Capers

Salt and black pepper

For the crêpe batter, in a medium bowl (or blender or food processor), combine eggs, ½ cup (125 mL) of the milk, water, flour, and salt. Beat at medium speed (or blend) until smooth. While beating at low speed, slowly pour in remaining milk. Add butter; beat at medium speed (or blend) until well combined.

Preheat oven to 200°F (100°C). Heat a medium skillet or crêpe pan over medium-high heat until hot. Using a paper towel, lightly coat pan with melted butter. Pour a paper-thin layer of batter into pan, swirling pan to coat bottom. Cook until crêpe looks almost dry on top and slides when pan is shaken, about 3 minutes. Flip and cook until golden brown spots appear on the bottom, about 30 seconds. Transfer crêpe to a plate; cover with foil and keep warm in oven. Repeat with remaining batter, wiping pan with additional butter as needed, and stacking finished crêpes.

For the crêpe filling, in a bowl, beat cream cheese with mayonnaise. Spread mixture down middle of each crêpe. Top each crêpe with smoked salmon, 2 slices of tomato, onion, roasted peppers, green peppers, capers, and salt and pepper to taste. Roll crêpes to enclose filling.

Many chefs think of their food as art, but at La Dominique Creperie the chef was indeed a professional sculptor before opening his food truck. In a four-by-eight trailer in Philadelphia, Zbigniew Chojnacki takes great pride in his sweet and savory crêpes that people patiently wait in long lines for.

The food truck revolution is largely a rebellion against the mediocrity of fast food, and at La Dominique, you will find no better example of delicious *slow* food. This smoked salmon crêpe is one of the most popular items on the menu. Zbigniew took the classic cream cheese and lox on a bagel to dizzying new heights by switching the heavy bagel for a light crêpe. A small change, but a world of difference.

CHICKEN CHILI RELLENO POCKET PIES

Serves 12 to 15

A food truck is a small work environment, so it's important to know exactly what your job is, even more so when you are *married* to the person you share the kitchen with. Joe and Joanna of Oh My! Pocket Pies have perfected cramming themselves plus a lot of classic comfort food into their pocket-size gourmet bundles of goodness. Joanna looks after the sweet and dessert pies while Joe looks after the savory, and the result is lots of very happy, well-fed citizens of Houston.

Chicken relleno is a staple dish in the Longhorn State and can be found on most menus. And here it is in convenient handheld form. Oh my!

Pocket Pie Dough

6 cups (1.5 L) all-purpose flour
2 tbsp (30 mL) baking powder
¼ tsp (1 mL) garlic powder
Pinch of salt
1 cup (250 mL) shortening
1 egg
2 cups (500 mL) cold water

Chicken Chili Relleno Filling

2 to 3 medium poblano chilies
2 tbsp (30 mL) vegetable oil
½ cup (125 mL) finely chopped onion
1 lb (450 g) ground chicken breast
2 cloves garlic, minced

2 tbsp (30 mL) butter
¼ cup (60 mL) all-purpose flour
1 cup (250 mL) water
2 tsp (10 mL) ancho chili powder
½ tsp (2 mL) paprika
¼ tsp (1 mL) crumbled dried oregano
⅛ tsp (0.5 mL) ground cumin
Salt and white pepper
½ cup (125 mL) fresh or thawed frozen corn kernels
½ cup (125 mL) shredded Monterey Jack cheese
Juice of ½ lime
Cooking oil for deep-frying (optional)

For the pie dough, in the bowl of a stand mixer fitted with the paddle attachment, sift together flour, baking powder, garlic powder, and salt. Mix in shortening until mixture resembles fine crumbs. Beat egg with water; with the mixer on low speed, slowly add liquid to flour mixture. Continue to mix for about 5 minutes, until a firm dough forms. Wrap dough in plastic and refrigerate for at least 1 hour.

Meanwhile, make the filling. Roast poblano chilies directly over flame of grill or gas stove, turning frequently, until they blister and blacken. Let cool, then peel with paper towel. Remove stems and seeds; cut peppers into ½-inch (1 cm) pieces. Set aside.

In a large skillet, heat 1 tbsp (15 mL) of the vegetable oil over medium-high heat. Add ¼ cup (60 mL) of the onion; sauté for 1 to 2 minutes, until beginning to soften. Add ground chicken. Sauté just until chicken is cooked through; transfer to a large bowl.

In the same skillet, heat remaining 1 tbsp (15 mL) vegetable oil over medium-high heat. Add remaining ¼ cup (60 mL) onion, garlic, and reserved poblano chilies; cook, stirring, until onions soften. Add butter. When butter has melted, sprinkle mixture with flour, then stir to blend evenly. Slowly stir in water until mixture has a gravy consistency. Add chili powder, paprika, oregano, cumin, and salt and white pepper to taste; stir well. Cook, stirring, for 3 to 5 minutes or until gravy is desired thickness. Stir gravy into cooked chicken. Stir in corn. Let cool.

Stir Jack cheese and lime juice into cooled filling. Divide dough into 12 to 15 equal portions; roll each portion into a ball. On a lightly floured work surface, roll balls into disks about ¼ inch (5 mm) thick. Spoon mixture onto one side of prepared dough disks, leaving a 1-inch (2.5 cm) border; moisten edges of dough with water. Crimp with a dough press or fold dough over and press edges firmly with fingers.

In a deep-fryer or deep, heavy saucepan, heat 3 inches (8 cm) of cooking oil to 350°F (180°C). Working in batches, fry pies for 4 to 5 minutes, until golden on both sides. Drain on paper towels. (Alternatively, bake pies on a parchment-lined baking sheet in a 375°F/190°C oven until golden, 15 to 20 minutes.) Let cool before serving.

BEEF SHAWARMA WITH CHIMICHURRI SAUCE

Serves 5

Beef Shawarma

1 rib-eye steak (4 lb/1.8 kg)

1 cup (250 mL) olive oil

5 dried bay leaves

5 cinnamon sticks

¼ cup (60 mL) minced garlic

1 tbsp (30 mL) ground cardamom

1 tbsp (15 mL) ground cumin

2 tsp (10 mL) kosher salt

1 cup (250 mL) chicken stock

¼ cup (60 mL) lemon juice

Chimichurri Sauce

1½ cups (375 mL) canola/
    olive oil blend

¾ cup (175 mL) seasoned rice vinegar

¾ cup (175 mL) cider vinegar

½ cup (125 mL) lemon juice

1 tbsp (15 mL) kosher salt

½ tsp (2 mL) hot pepper flakes

½ tsp (2 mL) black pepper

¼ tsp (1 mL) white pepper

½ cup (125 mL) flat-leaf parsley
    leaves with very little stem,
    finely chopped

6 tbsp (90 mL) fresh mint
    leaves, finely chopped

¼ cup (60 mL) fresh basil
    leaves, finely chopped

For serving

5 pita breads

To marinate the beef, trim steak and cut across the grain into ¼-inch (5 mm) slices. In a nonaluminum bowl, combine oil, bay leaves, cinnamon sticks, garlic, cardamom, cumin, and salt; stir well. Add beef and turn to coat all sides thoroughly with spice mix. Marinate beef, covered and refrigerated, for at least 4 hours or overnight

For the chimichurri sauce, in a medium bowl, combine oil, rice vinegar, cider vinegar, lemon juice, salt, pepper flakes, black pepper, and white pepper; whisk until emulsified. Fold in parsley, mint, and basil; mix well. Let chimichurri sauce sit at room temperature for at least 30 minutes before using to develop flavors.

To finish the shawarma, preheat oven to 350°F (180°C). Spread marinated beef in a single layer in a roasting pan and cover tightly with heavy-duty foil. Roast until meat is no longer leaking juices but is still tender, about 10 minutes. Meanwhile, heat a large skillet over medium-high heat. Transfer meat and pan juices to skillet. When meat starts to sizzle, stir in stock and lemon juice. Serve shawarma in pitas with chimichurri sauce.

Washington is a city of embassies and international flavors, and keeping all those particular palates happy can be a challenge. Truck owner Farhad Assari's theory was this: "Food is basically proteins and carbohydrates, but it is the *sauces* you put on it that make the unique flavors." Sâuçá did just this by offering sixteen gourmet sauces made from scratch daily. Customers got to create their own dishes by adding their choice of sauce on the spot.

MAC AND CHEESE CONES WITH BACON "BLING"

Serves 6

The best part of eating macaroni and cheese out of a waffle cone is that you don't get an ice-cream headache! I don't think that's why Annemarie and Tom came up with the idea, but what a great happy accident. Known for its amazing seafood, Baltimore's Gypsy Queen Cafe is rolling around serving locals who can't get enough of their unique cones. The Mac and Cheese Cone is one of their most popular.

And what are gypsies without their bling? In this case we're talking not jewelry but *bacon* bling—an amazing sweet-tart-appley-smoky-bacony topping that's the perfect adornment for mac and cheese.

Bacon "Bling"

1 lb (450 g) bacon, diced

1 large red onion, finely chopped

2 tart apples, diced

3 cups (750 mL) barbecue sauce

3 tbsp (45 mL) liquid smoke

3 tbsp (45 mL) balsamic vinegar

Mac and Cheese Cones

1½ lb (675 g) macaroni, cooked and cooled

2 cups (500 mL) cream cheese, softened

1 lb (450 g) American cheese, cubed

8 oz (225 g) Asiago cheese, grated

4 cups (1 L) 10% cream

6 large malted waffle cones

For the "bling," in a large skillet, cook bacon, onion, and apples over medium-high heat until bacon is crisp. Stir in barbecue sauce, liquid smoke, and vinegar. Reduce heat to a simmer and cook until thick and caramelized, about 1 hour. Remove from heat.

For the cones, in a large saucepan, combine macaroni, cream cheese, American cheese, Asiago cheese, and cream. Heat over low heat, stirring frequently, until cheeses are melted and well blended. Spoon mac and cheese into malted cones and top with bacon "bling."

HOT & CRUNCHY CHICKEN CONES

Serves 4

Patrons of the Austin City Limits music fest had a problem: how could they eat their street food with one hand while balancing a beer in the other? Jeff Blank, owner of a swanky Austin eatery called Hudson's on the Bend, had an idea. Why not take some of the favorite menu items at his restaurant and serve them up in a handy cardboard cone? Apparently the idea was genius, because they sold 22,000 of them in three days!

The hot and crunchy batter is a tradition in the restaurant, but when you roll chicken in it and serve it up in a cone, it's what you call *some good eatin'*. The secret behind the crunchy batter? Cornflakes (where, ironically, the chicken is on the front of the box)!

Hot & Crunchy Mix

2 cups (500 mL) cornflakes
¼ cup (60 mL) slivered almonds
¼ cup (60 mL) sesame seeds
¼ cup (60 mL) sugar
4 tsp (20 mL) hot pepper flakes
1 tbsp (15 mL) salt

Ancho Paint

½ cup (125 mL) ancho or
    chipotle chili purée
Juice of 2 lemons
6 cloves garlic
2 shallots
2 cups (500 mL) mayonnaise
2 tbsp (30 mL) dark brown sugar
2 tbsp (30 mL) rice wine vinegar
Salt

Mango Jalapeño Sauce

1 lb (450 g) mangoes, peeled and
    diced (thawed if frozen)
1½ cups (375 mL) sugar
6 tbsp (90 mL) white wine vinegar
3 tbsp (45 mL) diced red onion
2 tbsp (30 mL) minced garlic
4 jalapeño peppers, seeded
    and sliced
½ tsp (2 mL) salt

Mango Jalapeño Aïoli

Leaves from 1 bunch fresh
    cilantro, roughly chopped
Juice of 2 limes
2 cloves garlic, minced
1½ cups (375 mL) mayonnaise
½ cup (125 mL) mango
    jalapeño sauce
1 tbsp (15 mL) salt
1 tbsp (15 mL) pepper

Jalapeño Slaw

4 cups (1 L) shredded
    green cabbage
2 cups (500 mL) shredded
    red cabbage
1 cup (250 mL) shredded carrots
2 cups (500 mL) mango
    jalapeño aïoli

Chicken

1 cup (250 mL) all-purpose flour
2 eggs
¾ cup (175 mL) milk
1½ lb (675 g) chicken tenders
⅓ cup (75 mL) clarified butter
    or peanut or canola oil

Cones

4 small flour tortillas
4 paper drink cones

For the hot & crunchy mix, in a food processor combine cornflakes, almonds, sesame seeds, sugar, pepper flakes, and salt. Pulse just until combined; the mix should be coarse. (Mix can be made several days ahead and kept in an airtight container at room temperature.)

For the ancho paint, in a blender, combine chili purée, lemon juice, garlic, shallots, mayonnaise, sugar, vinegar, and salt to taste. Blend until smooth. Using a rubber spatula, push sauce through a fine-mesh sieve, discarding solids. Transfer sauce to a squeeze bottle or jar. (Sauce can be made several days ahead and refrigerated.)

For the mango jalapeño sauce, in a large saucepan, combine mangoes, sugar, vinegar, onion, and garlic. Simmer, stirring occasionally, for 15 minutes. Stir in jalapeños and salt; simmer for another 3 minutes. Let cool, then chill well before making aïoli. (Sauce can be made several days ahead and refrigerated, covered.)

For the mango jalapeño aïoli, in a medium bowl, combine cilantro, lime juice, garlic, mayonnaise, mango jalapeño sauce, salt, and pepper; stir well. Cover and refrigerate for at least 4 hours or overnight.

Shortly before serving, make the slaw. In a large bowl, combine green cabbage, red cabbage, and carrots. Add aïoli; toss to coat. The slaw should be very wet. Refrigerate until needed.

For the chicken, preheat oven to 200°F (100°C). Put the flour in a shallow dish. In another shallow dish, whisk together eggs and milk. Spread the hot & crunchy mix in a third dish. Dredge chicken tenders in flour, shaking off excess. Dip in egg wash, coating thoroughly, letting excess drip off. Roll chicken in hot & crunchy mix, lightly pressing mixture onto chicken with the palm of your hand and coating thoroughly. Shake off excess. Set chicken aside on a baking sheet.

In a large, heavy sauté pan, heat clarified butter to 325°F (160°C) or until a sprig of parsley sizzles when tossed in the oil. Working in batches if necessary, carefully lay chicken in hot oil. Sauté for 3 to 4 minutes per side, turning once, until chicken is a golden, crunchy brown. Drain on paper towels, then transfer to a baking sheet and keep warm in the oven while you repeat with remaining chicken.

To finish the cones, in a skillet over medium heat, heat tortillas until warm but still pliable. Insert a warm tortilla into each paper cone. Fill with chicken tenders, followed by slaw and a healthy squirt of ancho paint.

SOUPS, NOODLES
& SAUCY THINGS

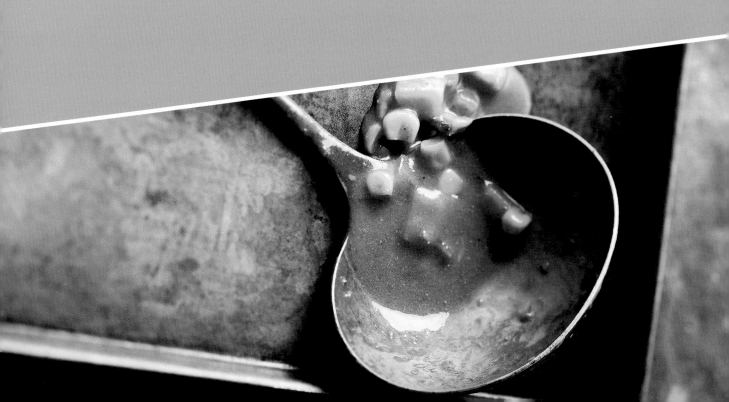

If I had a nickel for every time someone called me a saucy thing, I would have about...ten cents. But that really isn't the point. The point is, we're taking it to the streets now and kicking up the spice with our sassiest, sauciest trucks.

When you think of food trucks, soups and noodles aren't usually the first thing to pop into mind. But these chefs have such a passion for their chowders, curries, noodles, and gumbos that their curbside offerings are neck and neck with burgers and dogs. From chowders that are perfect for a chilly day to a cool Mexican gazpacho-like treat in the hot summer sun, from Thai curried scallops to Japanese noodles, this chapter brings these favorite curbside creations right to your own home.

SOUPS, NOODLES
& SAUCY THINGS

PACIFIC RIM CHOWDER

Serves 8

1 can (12 oz/341 mL) corn kernels

2 tbsp (30 mL) canola/olive oil blend

1½ cups (375 mL) finely chopped onions

1½ cups (375 mL) diced carrots

1½ cups (375 mL) diced celery

1½ cups (375 mL) diced parboiled potatoes

¼ cup (60 mL) crushed garlic

2 tsp (10 mL) toasted ground coriander

1 tsp (5 mL) toasted ground cumin

1 tsp (5 mL) sea salt

1 tsp (5 mL) pepper

1 can (14 oz/398 mL) crushed tomatoes

3 cans (each 14 oz/400 mL) coconut milk

½ cup (125 mL) sweet chili sauce

¼ cup (60 mL) chipotle chilies in adobo sauce, chopped

2 tbsp (30 mL) hot sauce

2 tbsp (30 mL) Worcestershire sauce

Leaves from 1 bunch fresh cilantro, minced

Sustainably harvested white fish or seafood (such as cod, halibut, shrimp, scallops, lobster), cut into bite-size pieces

Cilantro leaves and sliced green onions for garnish

Drain corn, reserving liquid. Heat oil in a large pot over medium-high heat. Add corn, onions, carrots, celery, potatoes, garlic, coriander, cumin, salt, and pepper. Sauté until vegetables are soft. Add reserved corn liquid, tomatoes, coconut milk, chili sauce, chipotles, hot sauce, Worcestershire sauce, and minced cilantro. Simmer for 10 minutes. Stir in fish; simmer for another 5 minutes or until fish is just cooked. Serve garnished with cilantro leaves and green onions.

Kunal Ghose and Simon Sobolewski's "food truck," Red Fish Blue Fish, has the ideal location—right in Victoria's beautiful Inner Harbour. So local are their ingredients, they could almost jump right out of the water at the end of the dock. These guys take sustainability so seriously that their kitchen and servery is in a recycled shipping container.

Their Pacific Rim Chowder is simply the best soup we've ever had from a food truck—or a shipping container. Locals consider this sophisticated twist on good ol' clam chowder ambrosia from the sea.

SOBA NOODLES

Serves 2

Who doesn't love dim sum, where carts of food come right to your table? Chef Chris Hodgson thought he would take that one step further and opened a cart that brings you food *wherever* you are in the city of Cleveland. Just one more reason why Cleveland rocks!

I'm used to having soba noodles served up in a hot broth, but Chris serves them chilled in a light summery style that's perfect for a weekend barbecue. In his words, these are "totally slurpalicious!"

1 lb (450 g) soba noodles

2 bunches mustard greens

2 cloves garlic, minced

6 tbsp (90 mL) soy sauce

2 tsp (10 mL) Korean chili flakes

2 tsp (10 mL) honey

2 tsp (10 mL) fish sauce

2 tsp (10 mL) sambal oelek

6 tbsp (90 mL) frozen shelled edamame, thawed

2 tsp (10 mL) thinly sliced green onion

Cook soba noodles in boiling water until tender, about 3 minutes. Remove with a skimmer or large slotted spoon and cool in ice water.

In same pot of water, blanch mustard greens for 4 minutes. Drain and cool in ice water.

In a small bowl, whisk together garlic, soy sauce, chili flakes, honey, fish sauce, and sambal oelek.

Drain noodles and mustard greens well. In a large bowl toss together noodles, mustard greens, and edamame. Divide noodle mixture between 2 bowls. Drizzle with sauce until it coats all of the noodles, edamame, and mustard greens. Garnish with green onion.

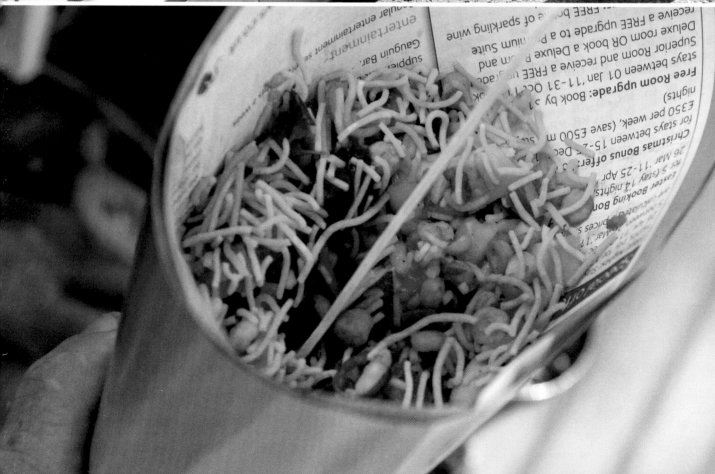

JHAL MURI

Serves 4

Tamarind Sauce

1 pkg (14 oz/400 g) pliable tamarind

1 lb (500 g) jaggery or palm sugar

11 whole cloves

11 cardamom pods

11 black peppercorns

3 star anise

1 whole blade mace

4 cups (1 L) water

Jhal Muri

¾ cup (175 mL) roasted peanuts
with skin

4 cups (1 L) muri (puffed rice)

¾ cup (175 mL) sev (crispy chickpea
flour noodles)

¾ cup (175 mL) chana dal
(fried lentils)

2 tomatoes, chopped

½ medium cucumber, chopped

1 small mild onion, chopped

1 cup (250 mL) mung bean sprouts

½ cup (125 mL) chopped fresh cilantro

¼ cup (60 mL) chopped fresh coconut

2 tbsp (30 mL) chopped fresh ginger

¼ cup (60 mL) tamarind sauce

3 tbsp (45 mL) fresh lime juice

4 tsp (20 mL) mustard oil

A few pinches of chaat masala

A few pinches of garam masala

Chopped fresh green chili for garnish

For the tamarind sauce, in a large saucepan, combine tamarind, jaggery, cloves, cardamom, peppercorns, star anise, mace, and water. Bring to a boil, then reduce heat to a simmer. Simmer, stirring occasionally to break up tamarind, for 30 minutes or until thickened. Let cool. Pour mixture through a sieve set over a bowl; squeeze solids with your hand to extract as much liquid as possible, adding a little more water if needed. Sauce should be the consistency of 18% cream. Discard solids. (Sauce keeps, refrigerated, for 2 weeks, or can be frozen.)

For the jhal muri, lightly crush peanuts; blow on them to remove skins. In a large bowl, combine peanuts, puffed rice, chickpea noodles, lentils, tomatoes, cucumber, onion, bean sprouts, cilantro, coconut, and ginger. In a small bowl, combine tamarind sauce, lime juice, mustard oil, chaat masala, and garam masala; stir well. Pour over dry mixture; mix well. Serve in a bowl or a newspaper cone, garnished with chopped chili, and eat with a spoon.

People always ask me what my favorite truck or cart is that we've featured on the show. Well, here it is. I don't know if it's Angus Denoon's personality, his skill as a chef, or the uniqueness of his dishes, but the Everybody Love Love Jhal Muri Express has to be the best example of true street food I have ever come across. Denoon astonished us with his style of Kolkata cooking. Don't let the simplicity of the Jhal Muri fool you. It's spicy, sweet, tangy, nutritious, and all-natural!

Chana dal can be found in South Asian grocery stores. To make your own, soak lentils for a few hours, drain well, then fry in 1 to 2 tbsp (15 to 30 mL) sunflower oil until browned.

PAD KEE MAO

Serves 4

When Wannee Hossain and her two sons, Bobby and Alom, decided to take their family's Thai restaurant mobile, they didn't do a food truck…theirs is a food *tuk*. Tuk-tuk is the slang for the auto rickshaws you find all over Southeast Asia. But none deliver food like Phat Thai!

The portion size of this dish may not seem like much in your kitchen, but by food truck standards it's huge, and it's one of many dishes that keep Phat Thai customers coming back again and again. This is the kind of delicious blend of crunchy vegetables and soft noodles that makes the texture of Thai cooking one of my favorites, and so far I haven't found anyone who does it better than these guys.

3 tbsp (45 mL) vegetable oil
3 cloves garlic, minced
⅓ cup (75 mL) chopped Thai chili
2 tsp (10 mL) ground Thai chilies
½ lb (225 g) ground chicken
1 lb (450 g) wide rice noodles
2 tbsp (30 mL) oyster sauce

1 tbsp (15 mL) fish sauce
Pinch of sugar
2 cups (500 mL) blanched broccoli florets
1 cup (250 mL) blanched thinly sliced carrots
1 sweet red pepper, thinly sliced
1 sweet green pepper, thinly sliced

In a large skillet, heat oil over medium heat. Add garlic, chopped chili, and ground chilies; cook, stirring, until garlic is light brown. Add ground chicken; cook, stirring frequently, until chicken is white and almost cooked through. Stir in noodles, oyster sauce, fish sauce, and sugar. Cook, stirring occasionally, for 3 minutes. Stir in broccoli, carrots, and red and green peppers. Cook for 2 minutes.

YELLOW CASHEW CURRY

Serves 6

Yellow Curry Paste

2 or 3 stalks lemongrass
    (light parts only), chopped

6 yellow chilies, chopped
    (or 1 tbsp/15 mL hot pepper flakes)

5 cloves garlic, minced

4 kaffir lime leaves, chopped

¼ cup (60 mL) chopped shallots

1 tbsp (15 mL) minced fresh
    galangal or ginger

1 tbsp (15 mL) ground cumin

1 tbsp (15 mL) ground coriander

1 tsp (5 mL) turmeric

¼ tsp (2 mL) cinnamon

1½ tsp (7 mL) salt

Cashew Curry

3 tbsp (45 mL) cooking oil

4 to 5 cups (1 to 1.25 L) halved
    cauliflower florets and diced
    stems (from 1 head cauliflower)

1 to 2 sweet green peppers, cut in
    1- to 2-inch (2.5 to 5 cm) pieces

1 large yellow summer squash,
    halved lengthwise and sliced

¼ cup (60 mL) yellow curry paste

1⅓ cups (325 mL) unsweetened
    coconut milk

⅔ cup (150 mL) vegetable broth

Juice of 1 lime

Toasted cashews, cilantro leaves,
    and lime wedges for garnish

Steamed rice for serving

Chef Stephanie Morgan left behind her life in the New York financial markets and now brings smiles to the faces of meat eaters and vegans alike with her amazing food. The folks of Orange County are flocking to the Seabirds truck for its outstanding organic, vegan fare.

At Seabirds they make this curry with cauliflower, bell peppers, and summer squash, but you can also use russet or sweet potatoes, mushrooms, asparagus, peas, spinach, green beans, carrots, broccoli…almost anything works!

For the curry paste, in a blender, combine lemongrass, chilies, garlic, lime leaves, shallots, galangal, cumin, coriander, turmeric, cinnamon, salt, and a little water. Blend until thick and smooth. Drizzle in a little more water if needed.

For the curry, heat 1 tbsp (15 mL) of the oil in a large skillet over medium-high heat; sauté cauliflower until tender and charred on all sides. Remove from pan and set aside. In the same pan, with a little more oil if needed, sauté green peppers and summer squash until just tender. Set aside.

Heat remaining 2 tbsp (30 mL) oil in a large saucepan over medium heat. Add curry paste; cook, stirring, for 1 minute. Whisk in coconut milk, vegetable broth, and lime juice. Bring to a simmer, then reduce heat to low. Add reserved cauliflower, green peppers, and squash; cook until heated through. Serve over rice, garnished with toasted cashews, cilantro leaves, and a lime wedge.

SEARED SEA SCALLOPS

Serves 4

Home Skillet is one of those rare trucks that stands out. Co-owners Christie and Vinnie wanted their patrons to feel at home, so they added touches like their signature ironing board, cruiser tables, and potted plants. That and teaming up with local farmers was a recipe for success.

In addition to such hits as their deep-fried Brussels sprouts, the Seared Sea Scallops are a must-try. What makes this dish sensational is the green curry sauce: lemongrass, Thai chilies, ginger, and other flavors tied together with coconut milk. It's delish!

Green Curry Paste

4 Thai green chilies

1 shallot, chopped

2 cloves garlic

1-inch (2.5 cm) piece fresh ginger, peeled and chopped

2 stalks lemongrass (light parts only), chopped

2 kaffir lime leaves

¼ cup (60 mL) water

Curry

¼ cup (60 mL) vegetable oil

1 onion, thinly sliced

1 sweet green pepper, thinly sliced

1 sweet red pepper, thinly sliced

3 tbsp (45 mL) green curry paste

2 cans (each 14 oz/400 mL) unsweetened coconut milk

½ cup (125 mL) vegetable broth

Salt and black pepper

8 jumbo sea scallops

Steamed rice for serving

2 fresh basil leaves, torn; 2 fresh cilantro leaves, torn; and lime wedges for garnish

For the green curry paste, in a food processor combine chilies, shallot, garlic, ginger, lemongrass, and lime leaves; pulse until finely chopped. With motor running, slowly add water until mixture forms a paste. (Unused curry paste keeps, refrigerated, for 2 weeks or for 6 months in the freezer.)

For the curry, heat 2 tbsp (30 mL) of the oil in a large skillet over medium heat. Sauté onion and sweet peppers until softened, about 5 minutes. Remove from pan and set aside. Heat skillet over medium-high heat. Add curry paste; cook, stirring, for 1 minute. Stir in coconut milk and vegetable broth; season with salt. Simmer, stirring occasionally, until sauce thickens, about 15 minutes. Return sautéed vegetables to sauce; heat through.

Meanwhile, remove the small side muscles from scallops; rinse scallops with cold water and thoroughly pat dry. In another skillet, heat remaining 2 tbsp (30 mL) oil over high heat until almost smoking. Season both sides of scallops with salt and pepper. Add scallops to hot pan, one at a time, making sure they are not touching. Sear for 90 seconds per side, or until they have a golden brown crust on each side and are translucent in the center.

To serve, divide rice among 4 bowls. Top with seared scallops. Ladle curry over rice. Garnish with basil, cilantro, and a lime wedge.

COLD CUCUMBER SOUP

Serves 4

Iliana de la Vega and her husband, Ernesto, bought a house in downtown Austin with the intention of opening a restaurant. But city permits and plans took so long that instead they opened a food trailer—in their driveway! It's stories like this we love to feature on *Eat St.* because that is exactly what owning a street food truck is about: creative chefs thrown into circumstances beyond their control and still managing to deliver delicious dishes.

El Naranjo served some of the best pure Mexican cuisine you will ever taste. Apparently this cucumber soup is so good you can hear the cucumber "sing" (although personally I think it's the fried tortilla strips on top that make all the noise).

6 cucumbers, peeled and seeded
1 small clove garlic
1 to 2 serrano chilies, stems removed
3 cups (750 mL) Balkan-style plain yogurt
¼ cup (60 mL) extra-virgin olive oil
Salt

Leaves and tender sprigs from ⅓ bunch fresh cilantro
3 small corn tortillas
½ cup (125 mL) canola oil
Cilantro leaves or cilantro micro greens for garnish

Cut cucumbers into chunks. Place in a blender along with garlic, chilies, yogurt, and olive oil. Blend until smooth. Add salt to taste. Add cilantro; blend until well incorporated but not puréed (you should see flecks of cilantro). Taste for salt. Refrigerate until cold.

Cut tortillas in half, then cut each half crosswise into thin strips. Heat canola oil in a large skillet over medium-high heat; fry tortilla strips until golden and crisp. Drain on paper towels.

Serve chilled soup garnished with tortilla strips and cilantro leaves.

DIRTY BLACK-EYED PEAS

Serves 12

2 lb (900 g) dried black-eyed peas

1 lb (450 g) peppered bacon, diced

4 cups (1 L) chopped yellow or sweet onions

Salt and pepper

4 smoked ham hocks

5 to 6 cloves garlic, chopped

4 or 5 bay leaves

6 sprigs fresh thyme

18 cups (4.5 L) unsalted chicken stock (approx.)

Soak peas in water for at least 1 hour.

In a stockpot over medium-high heat, cook bacon until crispy, 10 to 12 minutes. Add onions; sauté for 2 to 3 minutes, until softened. Season onions with just a little salt (too much salt will cause the peas to break up during cooking).

Score ham hocks through skin and fat. Add to pot; cook, stirring occasionally, for 4 minutes. Drain peas; add to pot. Stir in garlic, bay leaves, thyme, and enough chicken stock to cover peas by 1 inch (2.5 cm). Season with pepper. Bring to a boil over high heat, then reduce heat to a slow simmer. Cook, uncovered, for 2 to 2½ hours or until peas are tender.

Remove hocks. Discard skin and fat. Remove meat from bones; finely chop meat and return to pot. Add salt if needed. Discard thyme sprigs and bay leaves before serving.

We had no idea what to expect when we heard about Ms. P and her...food truck. But in Austin, Texas, Ms. P's is serving up dishes so good they'll "make you want to slap yo' mamma"—her words, not mine!

If you have never had the southern delight that is black-eyed peas, this recipe—with smoked ham, peppered bacon, onions, and garlic—will make you wonder why you don't have it all the time.

JAMBALAYA

Serves 8

The Swamp Shack in Portland is bringing authentic Creole cookin' from the South and puttin' it straight in your mouth! Don't call owner Trey Corkern a chef, though. He prefers the term "cook," saying that the difference between the two is one very important thing: *attitude*.

Trey makes his giant pots of jambalaya with the traditional wooden paddle—which can also be used to paddle your boat home if your motor conks out in the swamp. (See, folks? This isn't just a cookbook—it's also a survival guide.) The best part of this jambalaya is how the rice absorbs all that delicious deep flavor.

½ cup (125 mL) butter
1 lb (450 g) alligator sausage
⅓ cup (75 mL) minced garlic
1 lb (450 g) boneless, skinless chicken thighs
⅓ cup (75 mL) Creole seasoning
1 onion, chopped

2 cups (500 mL) chicken stock
½ cup (125 mL) tomato sauce
5 cups (1.25 mL) converted rice
¼ bunch celery, chopped
1 sweet red pepper, chopped
½ sweet green pepper, chopped

In a large, heavy pot (preferably cast iron), melt butter over high heat until browned (be careful not to burn it). Add sausage, sliced; cook, turning, for 2 minutes. Add garlic; cook, stirring, for 2 minutes or until pasty. Add chicken; cook, stirring constantly and breaking up meat with a wooden spoon, until chicken is no longer pink, about 5 minutes. Halfway through cooking, stir in Creole seasoning.

Stir in onions; cook for 2 minutes. Add stock; bring to a boil. Stir in tomato sauce and rice; cover, reduce heat to low, and cook for 14 minutes.

Stir, then remove from heat. Let sit, uncovered, for 10 minutes. Stir in celery and sweet peppers.

CHICKEN AND ANDOUILLE GUMBO

Serves 8

2 cups (500 mL) canola oil

2 cups (500 mL) all-purpose flour

2 lb (900 g) andouille sausages, cut in half-moons

2 lb (900 g) boneless, skinless chicken thighs, diced

Salt and black pepper

3 large onions, finely chopped

2 sweet green peppers, diced

4 stalks celery, diced

2 tbsp (30 mL) minced garlic

4 quarts (4 L) chicken stock

3 bay leaves

2 cups (500 mL) diced tomatoes

2 cups (500 mL) sliced okra

½ cup (125 mL) Creole seasoning

½ cup (125 mL) Worcestershire sauce

Hot sauce

Sherry vinegar (optional)

Steamed rice for serving

In a large, heavy pot (preferably cast iron), heat oil almost to the smoking point. (Oil will shimmer, and a pinch of flour will bubble.) Whisking constantly, add flour; oil will bubble and settle quickly. Keep whisking until roux is a nice café au lait color, about 30 minutes. Remove from heat and let cool.

In a stockpot over medium-high heat, sauté sausages until browned all over. Using a slotted spoon, transfer sausages to a bowl. Drain all but 2 tbsp (30 mL) of the oil. Sprinkle chicken with salt and pepper; sauté chicken until browned on all sides; using a slotted spoon, transfer to bowl with sausages.

Drain all but 3 tbsp (45 mL) of the oil. Add onion, sweet peppers, and celery to pot; cook, stirring frequently, until softened and browned. (Reduce heat if vegetables start to burn.) Add garlic; sauté for 3 minutes. Return sausages and chicken to pot; stir well. Add stock; bring to a boil.

Whisking constantly, add cooled roux a little at a time; return to a boil. Stir until gumbo is a thick, stew-like consistency. Add bay leaves, tomatoes, and okra; simmer gently, uncovered, for 1 hour. Add Creole seasoning, Worcestershire sauce, and hot sauce and salt to taste. Discard bay leaves. Just before serving, you may want to add a couple of drops of sherry vinegar to brighten the flavor. Serve over rice.

Creole cuisine is a fantastic blend of French, Spanish, Italian, American, and Cuban traditions. And Chef Matt Lewis claims to have the hottest, hippest, and sexiest food truck in Seattle, serving original Louisiana Creole out of his truck, Where Ya At Matt. In New Orleans, "Where ya at?" is how you say "How you doing?" and Matt is doing just fine, thank you very much, with a huge following of fans.

Cook up a batch of Matt's famous gumbo, with chicken, andouille sausage, okra, sweet peppers, tomatoes, garlic, and of course Creole seasoning, and your guests will be saying, *"Oowee souple, ban mwen."* (I think that loosely translates as: "I love *Eat St.*")

CUBAN BOWL WITH TOSTONES

Serves 12

On our travels we've seen a lot of things done with pork, but the folks at Snout & Co. bring new meaning to the phrase "pigging out." It's no secret why this truck's food is so good. The effort, time, and love that Chef Lee Scott puts into each menu item is obvious in every bite.

Scott's passion really comes through in his Cuban Bowl, which expands on an authentic recipe that came down from his grandmother. He lovingly soaks the beans overnight and then cooks them for about four hours on the truck. Then and only then does he jump in with the kick: garlic, oregano, cinnamon, and cider vinegar. Oh my! Grandma would be so proud.

Cushion Meat

10 cloves garlic, minced
2 cups (500 mL) orange juice
1 cup (250 mL) lemon juice
1 cup (250 mL) lime juice
¼ cup (60 mL) extra-virgin olive oil
3 tbsp (45 mL) pepper
3 tbsp (45 mL) dried oregano
2 tbsp (30 mL) ground cumin
3 lb (1.35 kg) pork cushion meat
2 tbsp (30 mL) packed dark
    brown sugar
Kosher salt

Black Beans

1 lb (450 g) dried black beans
¼ cup (60 mL) extra-virgin olive oil
3 red onions, finely chopped
4 sweet green peppers, diced
6 cloves garlic, minced
3 tbsp (45 mL) kosher salt
2 tbsp (30 mL) black pepper

3 tbsp (45 mL) dried oregano
2 bay leaves
3 tbsp (45 mL) cider vinegar
2 tsp (10 mL) sugar
1 tsp (5 mL) cinnamon

Tomatillo Coconut Sauce

1 lb (450 g) tomatillos, husked
½ cup (125 mL) sweetened
    shredded coconut
2 tbsp (30 mL) sugar

Tostones

Canola oil for deep-frying
12 green plantains, peeled and cut
    in 1-inch (2.5 cm) rounds

For serving

4 cups (1 L) steamed jasmine rice

For the cushion meat, in a large bowl or resealable plastic bag, combine garlic, orange juice, lemon juice, lime juice, oil, pepper, oregano, and cumin. Add pork, turning to coat. Marinate, refrigerated, for 10 to 12 hours. (Meanwhile, soak black beans and make tomatillo coconut sauce.)

Preheat oven to 225°F (110°C). Remove pork from marinade (reserving marinade, refrigerated); place in a roasting pan. Cover tightly with foil. Roast for 6 hours. (Begin cooking beans after pork has roasted for 3 hours.)

Transfer pork to a cutting board, tent loosely with foil, and let rest for 15 minutes. Increase oven temperature to 375°F (190°C); drain pan juices. Using 2 forks, pull pork apart; return to pan. Stir marinade into pork. Sprinkle with brown sugar and kosher salt to taste. Roast, uncovered, for 12 minutes. Cover loosely with foil to keep warm.

For the black beans, in a medium saucepan, soak beans in enough water to cover for at least 12 hours. Drain beans, return to saucepan, and add enough water to cover by 1 inch (2.5 cm). Bring to a boil, then reduce heat to a simmer.

Heat oil in a large skillet over medium-high heat. Add onions and sweet peppers; sauté for 2 minutes. Stir in garlic, salt, black pepper, oregano, and bay leaves. Cook, stirring frequently, until onions are translucent. Add onions to beans; stir in vinegar, sugar, and cinnamon. Simmer for 3 hours or until beans are soft.

For the tomatillo coconut sauce, prepare grill or smoker with cherry wood chips; preheat grill on high until chips smoke vigorously, about 20 minutes. Lower heat to medium. Smoke tomatillos at 225°F (110°C) for 90 minutes. Let cool. In a food processor, combine tomatillos, coconut, and sugar. Process until smooth. Set aside.

Shortly before serving, make the tostones. In a large skillet over medium heat, heat ½ inch (1 cm) of canola oil until hot but not smoking. Fry plantains, without crowding, until just golden, 2 to 3 minutes per side. Drain briefly on paper towels. With the bottom of a heavy saucepan, flatten plantains to ¼ inch (5 mm) thick. Return to oil and fry for another 1 to 2 minutes, until golden. Drain on paper towels.

To serve, stir together jasmine rice and black beans. Divide among bowls. Top with cushion meat. Place tostones in rice and drizzle tomatillo coconut sauce between tostones.

CURBSIDE
MEALS

Let's get down to the meals, the hearty, full-serving, sit-down main courses that you make for dinner. These dishes aren't fooling around. They are going to fill you up and put you in a food coma (and one of the trucks is even *called* that!).

Waffles, salads, pierogies, pastas, and pies—oh my, this is a fabulously filling section. Send out the invites and get ready to see some happy people!

The spices and flavors here come from all over the globe. Belgian, African, Mexican, and Russian are just a few of the cuisines you can add to your flavor passport. And the best part? Every one of these delicious dishes came from a food truck!

CURBSIDE
MEALS

LATE-SUMMER HARVEST SALAD

Serves 4

When I think of award-winning gourmet cuisine, I immediately think of Lansing, Michigan. At least, I do now! The Purple Carrot is a food truck run by boyfriend-girlfriend team Nina and Anthony, who obsess about turning local (and brightly colored) ingredients into fabulous menu items.

We don't see many salads on *Eat St.*, but wow, you gotta try this one! The sweetness of watermelon, the sour saltiness of the feta cheese, and the crunch of the pistachios make this salad a feast for almost every one of your senses, let alone your taste buds. Add heirloom tomatoes and this salad looks more like a Christmas tree than a healthy lunch!

Sherry-Maple Vinaigrette

1 cup (250 mL) extra-virgin olive oil

6 tbsp (90 mL) sherry vinegar

3 tbsp (45 mL) maple syrup

2 tbsp (30 mL) chopped fresh thyme

1 tbsp (15 mL) minced shallot

Salt and pepper

Salad

2 cups (500 mL) heirloom cherry tomatoes

2 cups (500 mL) watermelon balls (from about a 3 lb/ 1.35 kg piece, seeded)

½ cup (125 mL) crumbled feta cheese

¼ cup (60 mL) shelled unsalted pistachio nuts

2 Honeycrisp or Fuji apples, julienned

Smoked salt or other coarse sea salt

For the vinaigrette, in a small bowl (or jar), combine oil, vinegar, maple syrup, thyme, shallot, and salt and pepper to taste. Whisk (or shake jar) until emulsified.

For the salad, in a large bowl, toss together tomatoes, watermelon, feta, pistachios, and vinaigrette to taste. Serve topped with julienned apples and smoked salt.

CORN WAFFLES

Serves 10

1½ cups (375 mL) yellow cornmeal

1¼ cups (300 mL) all-purpose flour

½ cup (125 mL) sugar

1 tsp (5 mL) baking powder

½ tsp (2 mL) salt

2 eggs

2 cups (500 mL) milk

¼ cup (60 mL) canola oil

1 cup (250 mL) corn kernels

Preheat a waffle iron.

In a large bowl, combine cornmeal, flour, sugar, baking powder, and salt. In a medium bowl, beat eggs; stir in milk, oil, and corn. Stir wet ingredients into dry ingredients just until combined.

Pour enough batter into waffle iron to spread to edges; bake until crisp and golden brown and steam stops, about 5 minutes.

Serve waffles topped with vegetarian or beef chili, shredded cheese, sour cream, and fresh cilantro.

Wafels is self-explanatory, but *dinges* is Belgian slang for "toppings." And the toppings here go way beyond whipped cream and maple syrup, so much so that apparently Chef Thomas DeGeest is on the outs with many of his fellow Belgians for being so creative with the classic food of his homeland. When it comes to their food, the Belgians don't waffle. (Oh, come on. *That* was a good one!)

These slightly sweet corn waffles aren't the star of this dish. With vegetarian or beef chili, shredded cheese, and fresh cilantro on top, it's the *dinges* that make these *wafels* a full savory meal.

POTATO AND CHEESE PIEROGIES

Serves 8

How many Polish guys does it take to make a great food truck? One—as long as he has help from his Babcia! Stefania is Frank Giampa's grandmother. He loved her pierogies so much, he opened up Hoboken's only rolling pierogi palace and named it Stefania's Pierogi Truck.

You know you can't go wrong when you're using Babcia's old recipes, and the one that really won us over was the classic potato-and-cheese. Don't be too hard on yourself if you don't get the dough right the first time—it can take a bit of practice—but it is *the* essential element of a good pierogi. And don't forget to slather them with heaping spoonfuls of sour cream! *Bardzo dobre*, Babcia!

Pierogi Dough

6 cups (1.5 L) all-purpose flour

2 tsp (10 mL) salt

2 eggs

1 egg yolk

1 cup (250 mL) sour cream

1 cup (250 mL) water (approx.)

Potato and Cheese Filling

6 lb (2.7 kg) russet potatoes

1 tbsp (15 mL) butter

2 large onions, finely chopped

½ lb (225 g) farmer cheese

7 egg yolks, lightly beaten

Salt and pepper

For the pierogi dough, in a large bowl, stir together flour and salt. In a small bowl, beat eggs with egg yolk. Whisk in sour cream and ½ cup (125 mL) of the water. Stir wet ingredients into dry ingredients until dough comes together, adding more water if needed. Turn dough out onto a floured work surface and knead until soft and smooth. Wrap dough in plastic wrap. Refrigerate for 15 minutes.

For the filling, preheat oven to 180°F (85°C). Peel potatoes and cut crosswise into thirds. Put potatoes in a large saucepan, cover with water, and bring to a boil; reduce heat and boil gently until fork-tender, 20 to 30 minutes. Drain potatoes; spread in a single layer on a baking sheet and place in warm oven until all moisture has been released and no more steam rises. Transfer to a bowl; coarsely mash potatoes.

Meanwhile, in a large skillet over medium heat, melt butter. Fry onions, stirring occasionally, until golden, about 5 minutes. Reduce heat to medium-low; continue to cook onions, stirring occasionally, until soft and caramelized. Add to potatoes; add farmer cheese and egg yolks. Stir together well. Season with salt and pepper.

To finish the pierogies, on a lightly floured work surface, roll out pierogi dough to ¼-inch (5 mm) thickness. (Or use a pasta machine.) Using the rim of a glass or a 3-inch (8 cm) cookie cutter, cut out circles of dough. Place a generous spoonful of filling on each round; fold dough over into a half-moon shape and pinch edges together to seal.

Bring a large pot of water to a rapid simmer. Add pierogies; cook until pierogies float, 2 to 3 minutes. Drain well. (Alternatively, fry pierogies in clarified butter or canola oil until golden.)

BUTTERNUT SQUASH RAVIOLI

Serves 8 to 10

Ravioli is good, but fresh, handmade ravioli from a food truck is fantastic. It has made Zach Adams the undisputed Texas King of Ravioli. Ravioli so good it's regal! Adams learned to cook at restaurants along the Jersey Shore, where patrons do not take lightly to botched Italian dishes. As a result he is inventive but tries not to stray too far from the classic recipes.

In these ravioli, for example, he replaces the traditional Italian spinach with southern collard greens—a little thing with a big difference in taste. And there's so much more! The poblano chilies are sweet yet slightly spicy, and the creaminess of the butternut squash together with the cream cheese makes this a dish your Nona would be proud to serve.

Butternut Squash Filling

2 medium butternut squash

2 large poblano chilies

1 onion, finely chopped

Salt and white pepper

½ cup (125 mL) cream cheese
  or mascarpone cheese,
  at room temperature

⅓ whole nutmeg, grated

Pasta

2⅓ cups (575 mL) semolina flour

2 cups (500 mL) all-purpose flour

⅓ cup (75 mL) whole wheat flour

5 eggs

6 egg yolks

1 tsp (5 mL) salt

Fontina Velouté

4 tbsp (60 mL) butter

¼ red onion, minced

¼ cup (60 mL) all-purpose flour

2 cups (500 mL) vegetable stock

1 cup (250 mL) whipping cream

⅓ cup (75 mL) grated
  Parmesan cheese

⅔ cup (150 mL) shredded
  Fontina cheese

Salt and white pepper

Garnish

Chopped chives or
  green onions

For the filling, preheat oven to 375°F (190°C). Cut squash in half lengthwise and scoop out seeds. Place cut sides up on a baking sheet; roast until tender, about 75 minutes. Let cool slightly, then scoop out flesh. Purée in a food processor. Transfer to a large bowl.

Broil poblano chilies (or place over flame of a gas stove), turning, until charred on all sides. Peel, seed, and chop. Add to squash.

In a large skillet over medium-high heat, cook onion with salt and pepper to taste, stirring frequently, until caramelized. Drain well and add to squash. Add cream cheese and nutmeg. Stir mixture until well combined. Set aside.

For the pasta, in a large bowl, stir together semolina flour, all-purpose flour, and whole wheat flour; make a well in the center. Lightly beat together eggs, egg yolks, and salt. Add eggs to flour. Starting from inside edge, gradually incorporate flour into eggs until a soft dough forms. Turn dough out onto a lightly floured surface; knead for 10 minutes, adding more flour if needed, until dough is smooth and elastic.

Cover dough with plastic wrap and let rest for 15 minutes. (Meanwhile, make velouté.)

For the Fontina velouté, melt butter in a medium saucepan over medium heat. Add onion and cook, stirring occasionally, until soft. Stir in flour; cook, stirring, for 2 minutes. Whisk in vegetable stock a little at a time, then whisk in cream a little at a time. Lower heat to medium-low; stirring constantly, add Parmesan and Fontina a little at a time, stirring until melted. Season with salt and pepper. Set aside, keeping warm.

To finish the ravioli, on a lightly floured work surface, roll out pasta to ⅛-inch (3 mm) thickness. (Or use a pasta machine.) Cut pasta into sheets the size of a large ravioli mold. Spoon about 2 tbsp (30 mL) filling into each pocket. Brush edges with water, top with a second sheet of pasta, and press together to seal. Remove ravioli from mold. (Or cut rolled-out pasta into 2 rectangles. Drop 2 tbsp/30 mL of filling along dough, about 1½ inches/3 cm apart. Brush pasta with water and top with a second sheet of pasta. Using your fingers, gently press between and around each mound of filling to seal. Cut ravioli into squares.)

Cook ravioli in a large pot of gently boiling salted water until they float, 3 to 5 minutes. Using a skimmer or large slotted spoon, transfer ravioli to a large bowl. Gently toss with velouté. Divide ravioli among warmed plates and serve garnished with chives.

COLLARD GREENS

Serves 4 to 6

There is street food and there is street theatre, and the Fojol Bros. of Merlindia in Washington have blurred the lines and blended *both*. Theirs is not a food truck so much as a traveling food circus consisting of a few trucks and a cast of cooks and characters that make it one of the most unforgettable dining experiences we've ever had.

The Fojol Bros. may not take themselves seriously, but they take their food very seriously. Ethiopian cuisine is bold, hearty, and delicious, and these spicy collard greens will entertain your eyes and tantalize your taste buds…just like the Fojol Bros. themselves.

2 lb (900 g) collard greens, stems and tough ribs discarded
2 onions, thinly sliced
1 tbsp (15 mL) corn oil
8 cloves garlic, chopped
4 plum tomatoes, sliced
2 jalapeño peppers, sliced lengthwise
Salt

Cook collard greens in boiling water until tender, 12 to 15 minutes. Drain well, then spread out on a baking sheet to cool slightly. Squeeze collard greens in your hands to remove excess water, forming balls. Cut balls into 1-inch (2.5 cm) cubes.

Cook onions in a dry skillet over medium heat, stirring frequently, for 8 minutes or until softened. Add corn oil and garlic; cook, stirring occasionally, for 5 minutes. Stir in tomatoes; cook for 7 minutes. Add chopped collard greens; cook for another 5 to 7 minutes, until heated through. Remove from heat. Stir in jalapeños and season with salt.

EGGPLANT PARMESAN

Serves 6

2 eggplants

4 eggs

2 cups (500 mL) dry bread crumbs

¼ cup (60 mL) olive oil

¼ cup (60 mL) vegetable oil

1 lb (450 g) mozzarella cheese, shredded

2 cups (500 mL) tomato sauce

Preheat oven to 375°F (190°C).

Peel eggplants lengthwise for a striped look. Cut eggplants crosswise into thin rounds. In a shallow dish, beat eggs. Put bread crumbs in another shallow dish. Dip eggplant rounds in egg, letting excess drip off, then dredge in bread crumbs, coating thoroughly.

Stir together olive oil and vegetable oil. In a large skillet over medium-high heat, heat enough oil to cover bottom of pan. Working in batches, fry eggplant, turning once, until golden brown on both sides. Drain on paper towels. Add more oil to pan between batches if necessary.

In a 13- × 9-inch (3.5 L) baking dish, arrange 6 eggplant rounds. Top with some of the mozzarella and tomato sauce. Repeat layering until all eggplant is used, finishing with a layer of mozzarella. Bake until mozzarella is melted and hot, 20 to 25 minutes.

If you're going to open an Italian food truck in New York City, you better be good or you better get out of the way. But Johnpaul Perrone was so confident about his arancini, he told everyone he had the best balls in the city. That's confidence!

Perrone said he learned everything he knows about Italian cooking from watching his mother ever since he was a boy. One of her favorite dishes was eggplant Parmesan. It's pretty easy to make, but the secret here is in the sauce. Naturally Johnpaul wouldn't divulge his mom's secret recipe (not that we would expect him to), so feel free to play around with the tomato sauce to turn this into one of your own favorites.

KIMCHI QUESADILLA

Serves 5

Kimchi

½ cup (125 mL) salt, plus
    extra for rubbing

8 cups (2 L) + 3 tbsp (45 mL) water

2 napa cabbages

⅔ cup (150 mL) sweet rice flour

2 onions, chopped

1 Asian pear, peeled, cored, and
    chopped

1¼ cups (300 mL) minced garlic

2 tbsp (30 mL) minced ginger

1 tbsp (15 mL) fish sauce

⅔ cup (150 mL) gochugaru (Korean
    red chili powder)

2 tbsp (30 mL) sugar

1 daikon radish, julienned

2 carrots, julienned

1 leek (white and pale green parts
    only), thinly sliced

2 green onions, thinly sliced

Salsa Roja

½ lb (225 g) tomatillos,
    husks discarded, rinsed

1 lb (450 g) plum tomatoes,
    halved lengthwise

3 onions, cut in chunks

1¼ cups (300 mL) kimchi juice

¾ cup (175 mL) gochujang
    (Korean chili paste)

Salt

⅓ cup (75 mL) sesame seeds

Vegetables

¼ tsp (1 mL) dried oregano

¼ tsp (1 mL) onion powder

¼ tsp (1 mL) garlic powder

¼ tsp (1 mL) ground cumin

¼ tsp (1 mL) paprika

⅛ tsp (0.5 mL) cayenne pepper

1 tbsp (15 mL) vegetable oil

½ sweet red pepper, julienned

½ onion, thinly sliced lengthwise

¼ cup (60 mL) corn kernels

1 tbsp (15 mL) sesame oil

2 oz (55 g) tofu crumbles

Salt and black pepper

Quesadillas

5 large flour tortillas

5 oz (140 g) Cheddar
    Jack cheese, shredded

1 tbsp (15 mL) vegetable oil

Sesame seeds for garnish

Having hosted *Eat St.* for several seasons, I am no stranger to the food coma, that state of bliss felt after you've eaten so much good food you need to lie down and have a nap.

    Jay Cho's Vancouver Coma Food Truck rolled *only* with that intention. His background is Korean, but he added in American and Mexican traditions and flavors—brilliant fusion!

Begin the kimchi 3 days ahead (or 5 days in cold weather). In a large bowl, stir together ½ cup (125 mL) salt and 8 cups (2 L) water until salt dissolves. Cut cabbages in half lengthwise. Add to salt water. Place a lid or plate over cabbages to submerge them; add more water if needed to cover cabbages. Let soak until cabbage loosens, 30 to 60 minutes.

Meanwhile, in a small saucepan, combine sweet rice flour and 3 tbsp (45 mL) water. Bring to a boil, whisking vigorously until consistency is like glue. Let cool to room temperature.

Drain cabbages. Rub more salt on cabbage leaf by leaf, salting outer layers less than inner layers. Rinse cabbage under cold water and squeeze water from cabbage.

In a food processor, combine onions, pear, garlic, ginger, and fish sauce; purée. Add chili powder and sugar; pulse to blend. Add rice flour mixture; process to blend. Transfer to a medium bowl. Stir in daikon radish,

carrots, leek, and green onions. Stuff mixture between loosened cabbage leaves. Place in an airtight nonaluminum container and ferment kimchi at room temperature for 3 days (or 5 days if the weather is cold).

For the salsa roja, preheat oven to 400°F (200°C). Spread tomatillos and tomatoes in a single layer on a baking sheet. Roast until blistered, slightly charred, and softened, 15 to 20 minutes. Chop large pieces if needed. Meanwhile, purée onions in a food processor. Transfer to a large saucepan; stir in tomatillos, tomatoes, kimchi juice, and chili paste. Bring to a boil, reduce heat, and simmer for a few minutes, until onions are tender. Strain onion mixture, reserving liquid. In a food processor, purée solids, adding a little of the reserved liquid if sauce is too thick. Season with salt; stir in sesame seeds. Set aside.

For the vegetables, in a small bowl, stir together oregano, onion powder, garlic powder, cumin, paprika, and cayenne. In a small skillet, heat vegetable oil over medium-high heat. Sauté sweet pepper, onion, corn, and spice mixture until vegetables are just tender. Transfer to a bowl.

In the same skillet, heat sesame oil over medium-high heat. Add tofu, sprinkle with salt and black pepper to taste, and sauté until lightly browned.

For the quesadillas, cover half of each tortilla with half of the Cheddar, some vegetables, tofu, and kimchi. Top with remaining Cheddar. Fold tortillas in half. Heat oil in a large skillet over high until just smoking. Add a tortilla and reduce heat to medium-low. When cheese begins to melt, flip quesadilla. Increase heat to high for 20 seconds, then reduce heat to medium-low; cook quesadilla for 1 more minute. Remove from pan and keep warm. Repeat with remaining tortillas, adding more oil if needed. Cut quesadillas into wedges and serve garnished with salsa roja and sesame seeds.

BONZAI PRAWNS

Serves 4

Davis Bay, B.C., is one of the most pristine settings on earth, with the ocean right there, the clean, salty air—and a food truck. Before Feastro, most of the food trucks we visited were hard-core urban vehicles feeding hungry city dwellers. But we found Chef Steve Myddleton in a small town far from the nearest competition, serving up gourmet locavore cuisine. Feastro has become so popular that the city dwellers beg Steve to come visit more and more often… easy enough when your kitchen is on wheels.

These Bonzai Prawns are to die for. (Sorry, bad choice of words, but wow, are they good!) Cooking the prawns in white wine makes them slightly acidic and bitter, so the pineapple brochette lends a sweet helping hand.

Pineapple Brochettes

12 to 16 large fresh pineapple chunks
Olive oil

Prawns

¼ cup (60 mL) unsalted butter
2 cups (500 mL) sliced
    Bermuda onions
2 cups (500 mL) chopped tomatoes
¼ cup (60 mL) chopped
    flat-leaf parsley
2 tbsp (30 mL) minced garlic
Salt and pepper
16 to 24 prawns or jumbo shrimp,
    peeled and deveined
1 cup (250 mL) white wine
6 cups (1.5 L) cooked basmati rice
Cooked wild rice and cooked whole
    grains of choice
Chopped flat-leaf parsley and
    lemon wedges for garnish

For the pineapple brochettes, soak wooden skewers in water for at least 30 minutes. Preheat grill or broiler to high. Brush pineapple with oil. Thread pineapple onto skewers, 3 or 4 chunks per skewer. Grill, turning occasionally, until grill marks appear and pineapple softens, about 5 minutes per side. Set aside, keeping warm.

For the prawns, in a large skillet over high heat, melt butter. Add onions, tomatoes, parsley, garlic, and salt and pepper to taste; sauté for 4 minutes. Add prawns; sauté for 30 seconds. Add wine, cover, and cook for 2 minutes.

Arrange a small mound of rice and grains on each plate. Arrange prawns around the mound with tails pointing out. Spoon sauce over prawns. Add a pineapple brochette, and serve garnished with parsley and a lemon wedge.

THE SHRIMP MOFONGO

Serves 2

2 cloves garlic

3 tbsp (45 mL) canola oil,
plus extra for deep-frying

4 green plantains, peeled and cut in
28 (1-inch/2.5 cm) rounds

2 tsp (10 mL) white vinegar

Salt and black pepper

¼ cup (60 mL) diced
sweet green pepper

¼ cup (60 mL) finely chopped onion

¼ cup (60 mL) diced tomato

2 tsp (10 mL) tomato paste

24 small shrimp, peeled
and deveined

¼ cup (60 mL) shrimp
stock or fish fumet

1 fresh culantro leaf, minced
(or 1 tsp/5 mL minced
fresh cilantro)

Mince 1 clove of the garlic; set aside.

In a deep-fryer or deep, heavy saucepan, heat 1 inch (2.5 cm) of canola oil to 350°F (180°C). Fry plantains for 3 minutes or until light golden. Drain on paper towels for 1 minute. Using a cleaver or the bottom of a heavy saucepan, flatten plantains to about ¼ inch (5 mm) thick. Return to hot oil and fry for another 1 to 2 minutes, until golden and crunchy. Drain on paper towels.

Mash whole garlic clove in a mortar. Add 20 plantain chips, 2 tbsp (30 mL) of the canola oil, vinegar, and a pinch of salt and black pepper. Mash to a soft, silky consistency. Roll into 2 balls to create the mofongo balls.

In a small skillet over medium-high heat, heat remaining 1 tbsp (15 mL) oil. Sauté green pepper, onion, and diced tomato for 3 minutes. Add reserved minced garlic; sauté for 30 seconds. Add tomato paste; cook for 1 minute. Add shrimp, shrimp stock, and a pinch of salt and pepper. Cook, stirring, until shrimp is pink, about 3 minutes. Remove from heat and fold in culantro.

Place each mofongo ball in a bowl; spoon shrimp mixture over mofongo. Serve garnished with remaining plantain chips.

When brother-and-sister team Cindy Sierra and Sal Montalvo saw a need for an authentic Puerto Rican truck in Tampa, La Guaguita, or "the truck," was born.

Shrimp Mofongo is a tasty Caribbean dish that you just have to try. You might think the focus of the dish would be shrimp, but in fact the delicious plantain-based criollo sauce is what does all the heavy lifting here. Plantains love to be fried much more than their banana cousins because they are much more dense and contain so much natural sugar that they essentially caramelize themselves.

LOBSTER RISOTTO

Serves 4 (with leftover compound butter)

Compound Butter

½ lb (225 g) unsalted butter,
  at room temperature

Zest and juice of ½ lemon

1 tsp (5 mL) finely chopped shallot

1 tsp (5 mL) chopped garlic

1 tbsp (15 mL) chopped fresh tarragon

1 tbsp (15 mL) chopped fresh parsley

1 tbsp (15 mL) chopped fresh oregano

Salt

Lobster and Lobster Stock

2 live lobsters (each 1 to 1½ lb/
  450 to 675 g)

3 lemons, cut in half

2 onions, coarsely chopped

3 bay leaves

Salt

Risotto

2 tbsp (30 mL) grapeseed oil

1 shallot, finely chopped

2 tbsp (30 mL) chopped garlic

2 cups (500 mL) arborio rice

1 cup (250 mL) white wine

3 quarts (3 L) lobster stock

¼ cup (60 mL) compound butter

½ cup (125 mL) grated
  Parmesan cheese

½ cup (125 mL) mascarpone cheese

Salt

1 tbsp (15 mL) thinly sliced
  chives for garnish

Josh Martinez and Lyle Bento run a back-alley food trailer in Houston that cranks out off-the-wall dishes that would give Michelin five-star restaurants a run for their money.

If you go to a fancy restaurant you get a lobster. But at the Modular, for $22 you get a lobster *and* Lobster Risotto! Using the water the lobster claws are poached in as a stock for the risotto adds a sweet flavor you couldn't get from any other stock.

For the compound butter, in a bowl, combine butter, lemon zest, lemon juice, shallot, garlic, tarragon, parsley, and oregano. Mash with a wooden spoon or rubber spatula until thoroughly blended. Season with salt. (If using soon, keep butter at room temperature. Butter can also be made a few days ahead and kept refrigerated; bring to room temperature before using.)

For the lobster and lobster stock, place lobster on a cutting board. Place the tip of a heavy chef's knife behind the eyes; cut down through the center of the head. Remove each claw and knuckle (the large joint between the body and the claw) in one piece. (Set aside lobster tails for another use.) In a large pot, bring 2 gallons (7.5 L) water to a rolling boil. Add lemons, onions, and bay leaves; boil for 5 minutes. Add claws with knuckles; boil for 5 minutes or until shells turn bright red. Meanwhile, fill a large bowl with ice and cold water. Transfer claws and knuckles to the ice bath, reserving cooking liquid. When cooled, remove meat from claws and knuckles. Set aside meat and shells separately. Strain cooking liquid, discarding solids. Return liquid to pot, add reserved lobster shells, and bring to a simmer. Simmer for 20 minutes. Strain, discarding solids. Season with salt. Keep stock hot over low heat.

For the risotto, in a large saucepan, heat oil over medium heat. Add shallots and garlic; cook, stirring frequently, until softened but not colored, about 3 minutes. Add rice, stirring to coat; cook, stirring constantly, for 2 minutes or until you can smell the rice. Add wine; cook until wine is reduced by three-quarters. Add enough hot lobster stock to barely cover rice; cook, stirring, until stock is absorbed. Continue to add stock, enough to cover rice each time, stirring until each addition is absorbed before adding the next, until rice is almost al dente, about 17 minutes. Stir in ¼ cup (60 mL) of the compound butter, lobster meat, Parmesan, and mascarpone. Add a little more stock if risotto is too thick. Stir until rice is creamy and tender and lobster is heated through. Season with salt. Divide risotto among bowls and serve garnished with chives.

COCONUT HALIBUT CHEEKS

Serves 4

People are crazy about the Indian food at Vij's in Vancouver and Shanik in Seattle. Co-founders (and husband and wife) Chef Vikram Vij and Meeru Dhalwala wanted to find a way to serve the dishes enjoyed at railway stations in India. They came up with the brilliant idea of Vij's Railway Express, which is now roaming around Vancouver. Now we can all get a taste of Vij's mobile cuisine inspired by his annual food trips across India.

2 tbsp (30 mL) canola oil
1 lb (450 g) halibut cheeks (or spot prawns, peeled and deveined)
1 onion, finely chopped
2 serrano peppers, thinly sliced
1 tsp (5 mL) cumin seeds
1 tsp (5 mL) garam masala
1 tsp (5 mL) ground coriander
1 tomato, chopped
6 or 7 fresh curry leaves
2 tbsp (30 mL) balsamic vinegar
1¼ cups (300 mL) coconut milk
1 tbsp (15 mL) salt
½ cup (125 mL) chopped fresh cilantro
Steamed rice for serving

Heat half the oil in a large skillet over medium-high heat. Add halibut cheeks; sauté until golden, about 2 minutes on each side. Transfer to a plate and cover loosely with foil to keep warm.

In same skillet, heat remaining oil. Add onion; sauté until golden brown. Add serrano peppers, cumin seeds, garam masala, and coriander; stir until well mixed. Add tomato; cook, stirring, for a few minutes, until tomato begins to soften. Stir in curry leaves and balsamic vinegar. Stir in coconut milk and salt. Cook, stirring occasionally, until sauce is thickened, about 5 minutes.

Return halibut and any juices to sauce; simmer gently to heat through. Stir in cilantro. Serve over rice.

FISH AND CHIPS WITH TARTAR SAUCE

Serves 4

Tartar Sauce

¾ cup (175 mL) mayonnaise

¼ cup (60 mL) gherkins, finely diced

2 tsp (10 mL) capers, finely chopped

1 tsp (5 mL) finely chopped parsley

1 tsp (5 mL) lemon juice

Fish and Chips

Canola oil for deep-frying

2 cups (500 mL) all-purpose flour,
  plus extra for dredging

1 tsp (5 mL) baking powder

1 tsp (5 mL) turmeric

Salt and pepper

4 tsp (20 mL) vinegar

2 cups (500 mL) water (approx.)

2 lb (900 g) fresh skinless cod fillets

2 lb (900 g) large potatoes, peeled
  and cut in ½-inch (1 cm) sticks

For the tartar sauce, in a small bowl, stir together mayonnaise, gherkins, capers, parsley, and lemon juice. Refrigerate until needed.

For the fish and chips, preheat oven to 200°F (100°C). In a deep-fryer or deep, heavy saucepan, heat 2 inches (5 cm) of canola oil to 350°F (180°C). Meanwhile, in a medium bowl, stir together 2 cups (500 mL) flour, baking powder, turmeric, and salt and pepper to taste. Whisk in vinegar. Gradually whisk in water until batter is smooth but still thick enough to coat fish. Pour flour for dredging into a shallow dish. Dredge fish in flour, then dip into batter, coating thoroughly. Fry fish until golden brown on both sides, about 5 minutes. Drain on paper towels. Transfer fish to a baking sheet and keep warm in the oven.

Fry potatoes until golden brown, 7 to 10 minutes. Drain on paper towels. Season with salt and pepper.

Serve fish and chips with tartar sauce.

A food truck book has to include a killer fish and chips recipe, and this is it. The competition was thicker than fry batter, but the Frying Scotsman is the king…James King, actually—he owns the cart. King moved from Scotland and, on the advice of his wife, started up a cart in one of Portland's most popular food pods.

His fish and chips are so authentic that droves of British ex-pats flock to him daily for their fix. The extra-special kick is King's homemade tartar sauce. If you want to make it like James, skip using a blender.

SMOKED ALBACORE TUNA AND GREEN PAPAYA SALAD

Serves 4

El Gastrónomo Vagabundo is inhabited by Australian chef Adam Hynam-Smith and his Canadian partner, Tamara Jensen.

What a culinary and gastronomic journey! Proof? This salad, a blend of papaya, smoked tuna, and a delicious chili tamarind sauce. I guess that's the "vagabundo" part.

Tamarind water can be found in many Asian supermarkets. If you can't find it, soak 3 tbsp (45 mL) tamarind paste in ¾ cup (175 mL) hot water until soft; squeeze pulp with your fingers to dissolve it. Pour through a fine-mesh sieve, forcing liquid through with the back of a spoon and scraping pulp from the outside of the sieve.

Chili Tamarind Sauce

1 tbsp (15 mL) canola oil

4 red shallots, sliced

4 cloves garlic, sliced

1½-inch (4 cm) piece fresh ginger, peeled and sliced

4 long Thai red chilies, coarsely chopped

1 puck palm sugar (¼ cup/60 mL)

1 cup (250 mL) tamarind water

4 cilantro roots

Fish sauce

Seasoning Sauce

2 pucks palm sugar (½ cup/125 mL)

2 tbsp (30 mL) water

Fish sauce

Fried Shallots

2 tbsp (30 mL) vegetable oil

½ cup (125 mL) thinly sliced shallots

Green Papaya Salad

1 green (unripe) papaya, peeled, shredded, and bruised with mortar and pestle

8 cherry tomatoes, cut in half

½ cup (125 mL) fresh Thai basil leaves, torn

½ cup (125 mL) fresh cilantro leaves, torn

½ cup (125 mL) fresh Vietnamese mint leaves, torn

½ cup (125 mL) mint leaves, torn

Juice of 2 limes

For serving

1 lb (450 g) applewood cold-smoked albacore tuna, cleaned of sinew and thinly sliced

Finely chopped unsalted roasted peanuts for garnish

1 kaffir lime leaf, thinly sliced, for garnish

1 lime, quartered, for garnish

For the chili tamarind sauce, in a medium saucepan over high heat, heat oil. Add shallots, garlic, ginger, and chilies; sauté until starting to color. Add palm sugar and tamarind water. Reduce heat to medium-low. Stir until sugar is dissolved. Remove from heat and let cool.

recipe continued on page 202 . . .

Pour mixture into blender and add cilantro roots. Blend until smooth. Pour sauce into a bowl; add fish sauce to taste. Flavor should be a balance of sweet, sour, and salty. Transfer to a squeeze bottle, if desired. Set aside.

For the seasoning sauce, in a small saucepan, combine palm sugar and water. Stir over medium heat until sugar is completely dissolved. Remove from heat. Add fish sauce to taste. Flavor should be a balance of sweet and salty. Let cool completely.

For the fried shallots, in a small skillet, heat oil over medium-high heat. Sauté shallots, stirring frequently and being careful not to burn them, until deep golden, 4 to 5 minutes. Drain on paper towels. (Shallots will crisp as they cool.)

For the green papaya salad, in a large bowl, combine papaya, tomatoes, basil, cilantro, Vietnamese mint, and mint; toss gently. Dress with seasoning sauce and lime juice; toss gently to coat.

To serve, arrange tuna slices in middle of 4 plates. Top with green papaya salad, creating a pyramid. Squeeze 3 nickel-size dots of chili tamarind sauce around tuna (or drizzle with a spoon). Garnish with fried shallots, peanuts, lime leaf, and a lime wedge. Serve immediately.

CODFISH FRITTERS

Serves 4

1 lb (450 g) boneless salt cod

1 onion, finely chopped

2 cloves garlic, minced

1 small sweet green pepper, finely chopped

1¾ cups (425 mL) all-purpose flour

1 tbsp (15 mL) baking powder

½ cup (125 mL) mashed potatoes (optional, for thicker fritters)

1 tsp (5 mL) chopped fresh parsley

1 tsp (5 mL) chopped fresh cilantro

½ tsp (2 mL) finely chopped Scotch bonnet pepper

2 eggs, beaten

½ to ⅔ cup (125 to 150 mL) milk

Corn or vegetable oil for frying

Soak salt cod in water overnight (or boil for 20 minutes) to take out most of the salt.

Drain cod, then rinse in cold water. Squeeze water out, then flake fish by hand, removing any hidden bones. (They are fine, so do this step carefully.) Transfer fish to a large bowl. Add onion, garlic, green pepper, flour, baking powder, mashed potatoes (if using), parsley, cilantro, Scotch bonnet pepper, and eggs. Stir well. Stir in enough milk to make a batter.

In a saucepan or deep skillet, heat 1 inch (2.5 cm) oil to 350°F (180°C). Without crowding pan, drop batter by the teaspoon into hot oil, letting spoon touch oil so batter slides out smoothly. Batter should form a smooth ball and float in 15 to 20 seconds. Fry until golden brown, 3 to 4 minutes. Drain on paper towels. Serve hot with your favorite aïoli.

In music, riffs are phrases that deliver a constant beat or tone. In Music City, Riffs is a truck that consistently delivers delicious Caribbean-inspired food. Owners Carlos Davis and B.J. Lofback take pride in riffing off traditional Caribbean recipes, coming up with their own fusion creations. Carlos and B.J. met while feeding relief workers after the 2010 Nashville flood, and today they are spicing up the diet of the average Nashvillian.

These delicious codfish cakes are perfect for sharing. Riffs describes them as more of a savory, salty doughnut. Soaking the codfish overnight tenderizes the fish and removes most of the salt that the cod is cured in. I recommend adding more potato for thickness and to make them nice and fluffy.

MACKEREL WITH BEETS AND HORSERADISH DRESSING

Serves 4

1 lb (450 g) beets

1 tbsp (15 mL) sugar

1 tbsp (15 mL) + 4 tsp (20 mL) white wine vinegar

Salt and pepper

1 lb (450 g) Yukon Gold potatoes

2 tbsp (30 mL) butter

2 egg yolks

1½ tsp (7 mL) dry English mustard

¾ cup (175 mL) + 1 tbsp (15 mL) canola oil

1 tbsp (15 mL) creamed horseradish

4 mackerel fillets

Handful of mustard leaves

Preheat oven to 350°F (180°C).

Wrap beets tightly in foil and roast until tender, 30 minutes to 2 hours depending on size. Unwrap beets, place in a bowl, and cover with plastic wrap; let sit for 30 minutes. Slip off skins with your hands. Cut beets into bite-size pieces. In a bowl, toss beets with sugar and 1 tbsp (15 mL) of the vinegar. Season with salt and pepper.

Cook potatoes in boiling salted water until soft. Drain, place in a bowl, add butter, and lightly crush with a fork. Keep warm.

For the horseradish dressing, in a small bowl, whisk egg yolks with mustard and remaining 4 tsp (20 mL) vinegar. Whisking constantly, drizzle in ¾ cup (175 mL) of the oil until emulsified. Whisk in creamed horseradish. Season to taste.

Heat remaining 1 tbsp (15 mL) oil in a large nonstick skillet over medium-high heat. Season mackerel on both sides with salt and pepper. Fry fish, skin side down, for 3 minutes, then flip and cook for 1 minute more.

To serve, spoon some potatoes on one half of each plate. Spoon some beets beside potatoes. Top with some mustard leaves and a mackerel fillet. Drizzle with horseradish dressing.

It wasn't until *Eat St.*'s third season that we met the most aptly named truck we've ever encountered. Street Kitchen's classic American Airstream wouldn't get a second look on the streets of L.A. or Toronto, but for London, England, it is such an anomaly it borders on controversial! And for two of London's top chefs to abandon their high-end kitchens to toil away in a trailer is just…unheard of! The street food revolution is not as big in England as it is in North America, but Jun and Mark have captured every nuance, offering gourmet food at street food prices.

Their mackerel is top drawer, from the sweet-sour roasted beets to the smoothness of the creamed horseradish dressing.

GRILLED SWORDFISH AND GRITS

Serves 4

It's not that hard to bend a spoon, but we found a chef in Orlando who serves food so good, it will bend your mind! Steve Saelg calls his style "gourmet American continental," and you know he's serious about his cooking when you meet his sous-chefs. Trust me, not a lot of food trucks have sous-chefs.

Shrimp and grits is a dish you can find almost everywhere in the South, but Saelg ups the game by serving his grits with swordfish, a somewhat larger sea creature packed with nutrients and flavor. We've been to many food trucks and carts, and swordfish is not exactly a common item on menus. It's as rare as . . . sous-chefs!

Grits

2 cups (500 mL) 10% cream

2 cups (500 mL) water

1 cup (250 mL) white stone-ground grits

½ cup (125 mL) grated Parmesan cheese

4 oz (115 g) sharp Cheddar cheese, shredded

¼ cup (60 mL) unsalted butter

1½ tsp (7 mL) kosher salt

½ tsp (2 mL) pepper

Basil Vinaigrette

¼ cup (60 mL) basil leaves

¼ cup (60 mL) rice wine vinegar

2 tbsp (30 mL) honey

1 tbsp (15 mL) Dijon mustard

1 tbsp (15 mL) chopped garlic

1 tbsp (15 mL) chopped onion

¾ cup (175 mL) vegetable oil

Salt and pepper

Swordfish

4 swordfish steaks (each 4 to 6 oz/ 115 to 170 g)

Salt and pepper

For the grits, in a large saucepan, bring cream and water to a boil. Add grits, whisking constantly. Reduce heat and gently simmer grits, stirring frequently, for 10 minutes. Stir in Parmesan, Cheddar, butter, salt, and pepper. Cook, stirring frequently, for another 10 to 15 minutes, until grits are tender. Keep warm.

Meanwhile, preheat grill to high.

For the basil vinaigrette, in a bowl, combine basil, vinegar, honey, mustard, garlic, and onion. Using an immersion blender, blend into a paste. Drizzle in oil while blending. Season with salt and pepper.

For the swordfish, toss fish with ½ cup (125 mL) of the vinaigrette. Season with salt and pepper. Grill for 2 minutes per side.

Spoon grits onto plates. Top with swordfish. Drizzle with remaining vinaigrette.

SOCKEYE SALMON WITH SUCCOTASH

Serves 4

Succotash

2 tbsp (30 mL) olive oil

1 cup (250 mL) halved small Yukon
Gold potatoes, blanched

½ cup (125 mL) sliced onion

1 cup (250 mL) corn kernels

1 cup (250 mL) cooked chickpeas

1 cup (250 mL) cherry or teardrop
tomatoes

Zest of 1 lemon

½ cup (125 mL) fish or chicken stock

Salt and pepper

1 tbsp (15 mL) fresh thyme leaves

Vinaigrette

1 cup (250 mL) olive oil

¼ cup (60 mL) lemon juice

1 tsp (5 mL) fresh thyme

1 tsp (5 mL) Dijon mustard

1 tsp (5 mL) honey

Salt and pepper

Salmon

1 tbsp (15 mL) olive oil

4 sockeye salmon fillets
(each 6 oz/170 g)

Fresh herbs for garnish

For the succotash, heat oil in a large skillet over medium-high heat. Add potatoes and onions; sauté until slightly caramelized, about 5 minutes. Stir in corn, chickpeas, tomatoes, lemon zest, and stock; simmer until stock is almost gone. Remove from heat. Season with salt and pepper, then stir in thyme. Keep warm.

For the vinaigrette, whisk together (or shake in a jar) oil, lemon juice, thyme, mustard, and honey until emulsified. Season with salt and pepper.

For the salmon, heat oil in a large skillet over medium heat. Sauté salmon skin side down for 4 minutes. Flip and cook for 1 to 2 minutes more or until moist and flaky.

Spoon succotash onto plates and top with salmon. Drizzle vinaigrette over salmon and serve garnished with herbs.

Skillet Street Food is a classic American Airstream trailer converted to a gourmet kitchen that dishes out distinctive products like their signature Bacon Jam. Chef Josh Henderson and his crew, much like their trailer, can be described as "modern American," and this Sockeye Salmon with Succotash is a prime example of their style—that is, in the words of Josh, "simple dishes using good ingredients and not effing around with them that much."

SOUTHERN FRIED CHICKEN

Serves 4

There's Buzz and then there is Bee, and together they are the husband-wife team that brought soul food and southern fusion to Phoenix. Christian Buze ("Chef Buzz") and Beatrice "Bee" Bullock decided to step away from their jobs and venture into the food truck business. Their food was so good they quickly created quite a (wait for it…) buzz. All you need to know about what this truck is about can be found in the ever-popular Southern Fried Chicken.

The brine is what makes this chicken stand out in the hive. Not only is the meat lovingly marinated for 24 hours so the seasoning permeates deep into it but the spicy coating ensures this chicken is packed with flavor inside and out.

1 broiler-fryer chicken (2½ to 3 lb/ 1 to 1.35 kg), cut into 8 pieces
½ tsp (2 mL) garlic salt
½ tsp (2 mL) kosher salt
1½ tsp (7 mL) coarsely ground pepper
½ cup (125 mL) all-purpose flour
2 tsp (10 mL) paprika
2 tsp (10 mL) sea salt
1 tsp (5 mL) California or other mild chili powder
½ tsp (2 mL) garlic powder
½ tsp (2 mL) onion powder
Canola oil for deep-frying

Brine the chicken the day before. Place chicken pieces in a large bowl. Add garlic salt, kosher salt, and ½ tsp (2 mL) of the pepper. Add enough water to just cover chicken. Cover and refrigerate for 24 hours.

Preheat oven to 200°F (100°C). Drain chicken. In a bowl, stir together flour, paprika, sea salt, chili powder, garlic powder, onion powder, and remaining 1 tsp (5 mL) pepper.

Heat ½ inch (1 cm) oil in a large skillet over medium-high heat for 10 to 12 minutes to make sure oil is hot. Dredge 4 pieces of chicken in seasoned flour, shaking off excess. Carefully add chicken to hot oil. Fry for 6 minutes. Flip chicken pieces and fry for another 6 minutes. Continue to fry chicken, flipping every 6 minutes, until chicken is crispy and golden brown, 18 to 21 minutes. To test, poke chicken with a fork all the way to the bone; if no juices come out, chicken is done. Transfer chicken to a rack set over a baking sheet to drain; transfer to oven to keep warm. Repeat with remaining chicken. Let chicken rest for 5 to 8 minutes before serving.

LEMON CHICKEN COUSCOUS

Serves 4 to 6

Many chefs will tell you that offering your customers too many choices is asking for trouble because they'll never make up their minds. There is a truck in New York City where you can get your grilled meats one of three ways: on a sandwich, over rice, or over couscous. Chef Samir Afrit named his truck Comme Ci Comme Ça for just that reason—you can have your food "like this or like that."

Born and raised in Casablanca, Samir now offers the tastes of his homeland in the streets of New York. The Lemon Chicken Couscous is his number one seller because every delicious bite is like a trip to Morocco. Do what I do and enjoy it all three ways!

Lemon Chicken

4 boneless, skinless chicken breasts
½ cup (125 mL) lemon juice
¼ cup (60 mL) olive oil
1 tbsp (15 mL) dried oregano
1 tbsp (15 mL) dried thyme
1 tbsp (15 mL) pepper
1½ tsp (7 mL) salt
½ preserved lemon, finely chopped

Vegetables and Sauce

1 large onion, coarsely chopped
2 tomatoes, peeled and coarsely chopped
¼ cup (60 mL) vegetable oil
1 tsp (5 mL) olive oil
4 tsp (20 mL) salt
1½ tsp (7 mL) pepper
1 tsp (5 mL) ground ginger
½ tsp (2 mL) turmeric
½ handful of fresh parsley leaves, chopped
½ handful of fresh cilantro leaves, chopped
1 cup (250 mL) chickpeas, soaked overnight and drained

8 cups (2 L) water
6 carrots, peeled and halved lengthwise
3 turnips, peeled and halved lengthwise
2 or 3 small sweet potatoes, peeled and halved lengthwise (optional)
4 or 5 small zucchini (long or round), halved lengthwise
1 small butternut squash, quartered (or a small section of pumpkin, peeled and cut into 3-inch/ 8 cm pieces)

Couscous

3 cups (750 mL) water
1 tbsp (15 mL) salted butter
1 tbsp (15 mL) olive oil
1½ tsp (7 mL) cinnamon
1½ tsp (7 mL) turmeric
¼ tsp (1 mL) salt
3 cups (750 mL) couscous

To marinate the chicken, cut chicken into bite-size pieces. In a large bowl, whisk together lemon juice, olive oil, oregano, thyme, pepper, and salt. Stir in preserved lemon and chicken, turning to coat chicken thoroughly. Cover and refrigerate for 2 hours. (Meanwhile, make the vegetables and sauce. Soak bamboo skewers in water for at least 30 minutes.)

For the vegetables and sauce, in a large saucepan, combine onion, tomatoes, vegetable oil, olive oil, salt, pepper, ginger, and turmeric. Cook over medium-high heat, stirring occasionally, for 15 minutes or until browned and onions and tomatoes have formed a thick sauce. Add parsley, cilantro, chickpeas, and water. Cover and bring to a boil over high heat. Reduce heat to medium and simmer rapidly for 30 minutes.

Add carrots, turnips, and sweet potatoes (if using); simmer for 15 minutes. Add zucchini and butternut squash; simmer for another 25 minutes or until vegetables are tender. Adjust seasoning—sauce should be salty and peppery. Set aside, keeping warm.

Preheat grill to high. Thread chicken onto skewers (reserving marinade).

For the couscous, in a large saucepan, combine water, butter, oil, cinnamon, turmeric, and salt. Bring to a boil, then remove from heat. Stir in couscous. Cover and let stand for 10 minutes. (Meanwhile, grill chicken.) Fluff couscous with a fork to break up any clumps.

Grill chicken, basting frequently with marinade and turning occasionally, until chicken is no longer pink inside, 7 to 10 minutes. Remove chicken from skewers.

Divide couscous among plates, shaping it into a mound with a well in the center. Spoon vegetables into well. Arrange lemon chicken over and around vegetables. Spoon sauce evenly over couscous and vegetables. Serve with remaining sauce on the side.

JERK CHICKEN

Serves 8

Chef Troy Thomas's truck, the Rolling Stove, is hot, really hot. Hot as in popular and hot in that it serves up some of the spiciest jerk chicken, pork, and beef around Miami. This truck goes through five gallons of homemade jerk sauce *a week*, so you understand why Troy is known as the "King Jerk." He slaps this stuff on everything. We don't think you'll go through five gallons of sauce, but we know you'll be making this again and again.

Jerk Rub

¾ cup (175 mL) dark brown sugar
6 tbsp (90 mL) onion powder
⅓ cup (75 mL) salt
¼ cup (60 mL) garlic powder
3 tbsp (45 mL) black pepper
3 tbsp (45 mL) ground allspice
4 tsp (20 mL) cayenne pepper
4 tsp (20 mL) nutmeg
4 tsp (20 mL) ground thyme
2½ tsp (12 mL) cinnamon
2½ tsp (12 mL) ground sage
1 tsp (5 mL) ground ginger
1 tsp (5 mL) jalapeño powder
1 tsp (5 mL) habanero powder
1 tbsp (15 mL) orange zest
1 tsp (5 mL) lime zest

Jerk Marinade

4 large onions, coarsely chopped
2 bunches green onions, chopped
4 jalapeño or habanero peppers, chopped
3 cups (750 mL) white vinegar
2 cups (500 mL) orange juice
⅓ cup (75 mL) lime juice
1½ cups (375 mL) soy sauce

1 cup (250 mL) Jamaican rum
1 cup (250 mL) olive oil
½ cup (125 mL) granulated sugar
⅓ cup (75 mL) dark brown sugar
2 tbsp (30 mL) cayenne pepper
2 tbsp (30 mL) ground allspice
2 tbsp (30 mL) ground thyme
2 tbsp (30 mL) black pepper
2½ tsp (12 mL) ground sage
1 tsp (5 mL) cinnamon
1 tsp (5 mL) nutmeg

Barbecue Sauce

4 cups (1 L) store-bought vinegar-based barbecue sauce
2 cups (500 mL) orange blossom or other honey

Jerk Chicken

2 lb (900 g) boneless, skinless chicken thighs
2 tbsp (30 mL) canola oil

For the jerk rub, combine all ingredients. (Rub keeps, refrigerated, for several weeks.)

For the jerk marinade, in a large saucepan, combine onions, green onions, jalapeños, vinegar, orange juice, lime juice, soy sauce, rum, olive oil, granulated sugar, brown sugar, cayenne, allspice, thyme, black pepper, sage, cinnamon, and nutmeg. Simmer, covered and stirring occasionally, for 1½ hours or until onions are very tender. Let cool to room temperature. In batches, purée marinade in a blender. Set aside half the marinade for the barbecue sauce. (Marinade keeps, covered and refrigerated, for 1 month.)

For the barbecue sauce, in a large bowl, combine reserved marinade, vinegar-based barbecue sauce, and honey. (Barbecue sauce keeps, covered and refrigerated, for 1 month.)

For the jerk chicken, generously rub chicken with jerk rub. In a large pot or Dutch oven, heat oil over medium-high heat. Sauté chicken in batches, turning occasionally, until chicken is firm but not cooked all the way through. (Chicken may also be grilled.) Transfer chicken to a strainer and let sit for 30 minutes to drain off as much juice as possible. Wipe out pot; return chicken to pot and pour in enough jerk marinade to come one-quarter of the way up the chicken. Pour in enough barbecue sauce to come three-quarters of the way up the chicken. Simmer, uncovered and stirring occasionally, for 45 minutes or until chicken starts to fall apart. Transfer chicken to a strainer set over a bowl and let sit for 15 minutes. Return drained juices to pot; bring to a gentle boil and reduce sauce by one-quarter. Meanwhile, use forks to pull chicken apart. Stir chicken into sauce; heat through. Serve over rice or on buns.

CHICKEN TIKKA

Serves 10

Yogurt Sauce

2 cups (500 mL) plain yogurt

⅛ tsp (0.5 mL) kala namak (black salt)

Pinch of ground coriander

Pinch of ground cumin

Dash of sriracha sauce

Chicken Tikka

¼ cup (60 mL) chopped onion

¼ cup (60 mL) chopped garlic

¼ cup (60 mL) chopped fresh ginger

2 cups (500 mL) plain yogurt

2 tsp (10 mL) red food color (optional)

1 tsp (5 mL) cornstarch

1 tsp (5 mL) toasted cumin seeds

1 tsp (5 mL) toasted coriander seeds

1 tsp (5 mL) red chili powder

½ tsp (2 mL) ground cloves

½ tsp (2 mL) ground celery seeds

½ tsp (2 mL) salt

10 lb (4.5 kg) boneless, skinless chicken breasts or thighs, cut in ½-inch (1 cm) cubes

Chopped fresh cilantro for garnish

For the yogurt sauce, in a small bowl, stir together yogurt, salt, coriander, cumin, and sriracha sauce. Refrigerate until needed.

For the chicken tikka, in a mortar, combine onion, garlic, and ginger; mash to a paste. In a large bowl, combine ginger-garlic paste, yogurt, red food color (if using), cornstarch, cumin, coriander, chili powder, cloves, celery seeds, and salt; whisk until well blended. Stir in chicken. Cover and refrigerate for at least 1 hour. (Meanwhile, soak bamboo skewers in water for at least 30 minutes.)

Preheat grill to medium-high. Thread chicken onto skewers. Grill chicken, turning frequently, until blackish-brown on the outside and no longer pink inside, about 15 minutes.

Serve with yogurt sauce and chopped cilantro.

A two-time winner of New York City's Vendy People's Choice Award for street food, Meru Sidker's Biryani Cart might be small, but he serves up big flavor. Biryani is an Indian comfort food, a mound of rice cooked with meat, seafood, or vegetables and flavored with any number of spices. And when I say spices, I mean spices! With a wink or a nod you can have your dish fired up with one of a number of homemade fresh sauces that you don't taste…you *feel*.

For his Chicken Tikka, Meru marinates the chicken in the spices overnight. We have suggested an hour or so in the recipe, but feel free to try it longer to really let the flavors absorb.

YASSA CHICKEN

Serves 6

Austin is a city with a lot of food trucks, but there is one among them that the *Eat St.* cast and crew all fell in love with instantly. Cazamance is a trailer that Chef Iba Thiam built with his own hands, and in it he prepares authentic West African cuisine that you simply cannot find anywhere else.

Yassa Chicken is a dish that in Senegal you would make exclusively for your favorite person, and rumor has it that this very dish made Iba's wife fall madly in love with him...so be careful who you serve it to. You can make this as spicy as you want with the cayenne, or play it cool by leaving it out.

2 lb (900 g) chicken pieces (white or dark meat)

4 onions, thinly sliced

2 sweet red peppers, thinly sliced

2 poblano chilies, thinly sliced

2 cloves garlic, minced

1 cup (250 mL) green olives, pitted and sliced

2 tbsp (30 mL) lemon pepper

1 tbsp (15 mL) Dijon mustard

1 tsp (5 mL) dried thyme

Salt

Cayenne pepper (optional)

1 cup (250 mL) olive oil

1 cup (250 mL) water

In a large bowl, combine chicken, onions, red peppers, poblanos, garlic, olives, lemon pepper, mustard, thyme, and salt and cayenne (if using) to taste. Add half the olive oil. Mix well. Cover and refrigerate for 30 minutes.

Preheat broiler or grill to medium-high. Remove chicken from marinade (reserving marinade); broil chicken until browned on both sides. Set aside.

In a deep saucepan or Dutch oven, heat remaining oil over medium-high heat. Add marinade; sauté until golden brown. Add seared chicken; stir well to coat chicken with marinade mixture. Add water. Reduce heat to medium and simmer, partly covered, for 10 minutes or until chicken is cooked through. Remove from heat and let sit for 1 minute before serving. Serve with rice, or on a wrap or bread bowl as "bunny chow."

KUNG PAO CHICKEN

Serves 4

2 lb (900 g) boneless, skinless chicken thighs, cut into 1-inch (2.5 cm) cubes

2 tbsp (30 mL) soy sauce

4 tbsp (60 mL) sesame oil

1 tbsp (15 mL) minced ginger

1 tbsp (15 mL) minced garlic

10 bird's eye chilies (or to taste)

2 cups (500 mL) bean sprouts

1 cup (250 mL) chopped celery

½ cup (125 mL) roasted peanuts

Steamed jasmine rice for serving

Kung Pao Sauce

¼ cup (60 mL) sugar

¼ cup (60 mL) water

¼ cup (60 mL) chicken stock

¼ cup (60 mL) soy sauce

2 tbsp (30 mL) rice vinegar

2 tbsp (30 mL) rice wine

1 tbsp (15 mL) hot pepper flakes

1 tbsp (15 mL) cornstarch dissolved in 1 tbsp (15 mL) water

In a bowl, combine chicken with soy sauce and 2 tbsp (30 mL) of the sesame oil; mix well to coat chicken thoroughly. Marinate, covered and refrigerated, for 2 hours.

Meanwhile, make the kung pao sauce. In a small saucepan, bring sugar and water to a boil, stirring to dissolve sugar. Boil for 1 minute. Stir in chicken stock, soy sauce, rice vinegar, rice wine, and hot pepper flakes. Bring to a boil; whisk in cornstarch mixture to thicken sauce. Remove from heat.

In a wok or large, deep skillet, heat remaining 2 tbsp (30 mL) sesame oil over low heat. Add ginger, garlic, and chilies; cook, stirring, until chilies are sizzling. Increase heat to medium-high and add chicken. Cook, stirring, until chicken is light brown and almost cooked through, 5 to 7 minutes. Stir in bean sprouts, celery, and peanuts. Stir in kung pao sauce, stirring until chicken is coated and cooked through. Serve on a bed of rice.

For years Houstonians were used to ordering Chinese food and having it delivered, but Arthur Peterson and John Wentworth have taken that idea to a whole new level. With their rolling truck Rice Box, they bring the entire restaurant to you! There are a few examples of fusion-esque flair, but for the most part theirs is classic old-school Chinese food served up American style.

Kung Pao Chicken is a dish we've all had a thousand times before, but these guys do it up with a few slight differences. First, they use dark thigh meat, which westerners find more flavorful but is contrary to your average Chinese joint. Second, substituting jasmine rice for the traditional white rice stands true to the truck's motto: "Powered by rice!"

POLLO A LA BRASA

Serves 4

A *sangucheria* is a Peruvian foodie hot spot where patrons can indulge in handheld wraps and sandwiches. So the name Sanguchon felt perfect when Carlos Altamirano opened the first *sangucheria* on wheels in San Francisco, bringing his native Peruvian sandwiches streetside. Carlos is so renowned in San Fran that when he was getting ready to open Sanguchon, two local bread makers were competing to provide his buns and rolls.

Pollo a la Brasa translates as "charcoal roast chicken," which sounds kinda ordinary—until you bite into that tender marinated chicken with the chili-cheese sauce and the Peruvian sweet pepper salsa. Then it isn't so basic anymore!

Panca Marinade

4 guajillo chilies, boiled until soft, seeded
1 tbsp (15 mL) canola oil
1 tbsp (15 mL) red wine vinegar
Salt and black pepper

Chicken

1 chicken (2½ to 3½ lb/1.125 to 1.5 kg), quartered
1 tbsp (15 mL) puréed ají amarillo or other hot chili
1 tbsp (15 mL) soy sauce
1 tsp (5 mL) ground ginger
1 tsp (5 mL) dried oregano
Salt and black pepper

Huancaina Sauce

1 tbsp (15 mL) chopped onion
1 tbsp (15 mL) olive oil
1 tbsp (15 mL) puréed ají amarillo
¼ lb (115 g) queso fresco (or feta cheese), crumbled
Salt

Salsa Fusion

1 sweet rocoto pepper, finely chopped
1 clove garlic, minced
1 cup (250 mL) huacatay leaves, chopped
½ cup (125 mL) huancaina sauce
Salt

Watercress Salad

2 bunches watercress, tough stems discarded
Lime juice
White wine or sherry vinegar
Salt and pepper

For serving

4 sourdough buns, halved horizontally
French fries

Marinate chicken the day before. For the panca marinade, in a blender, purée chilies, oil, vinegar, and salt and black pepper to taste. You should have ½ cup (125 mL) marinade. Set aside. Rinse chicken, pat dry, and cut off excess fat. In a small bowl, stir together puréed chili, soy sauce, ginger, oregano, and salt and black pepper to taste. Rub seasoning all over chicken and under skin. Put chicken in a resealable plastic bag; add panca marinade, turning to coat. Marinate, refrigerated, overnight.

For the huancaina sauce, in a blender, combine onion, oil, puréed chilies, and cheese; blend until smooth and thicker than whipping cream. Season with salt.

For the salsa fusion, in a bowl, combine rocoto pepper, garlic, huacatay leaves, and huancaina sauce; stir well. Season with salt.

Preheat oven to 500°F (260°C). Arrange chicken skin side up in a 13- × 9-inch (3 L) baking pan. Pour 1 cup (250 mL) water around chicken. Roast for 30 minutes. Tent loosely with foil and roast until browned, about 15 minutes more. Transfer chicken to a cutting board; pull meat from bones.

Shortly before serving, make the watercress salad. In a bowl, toss watercress with lime juice, vinegar, salt, and pepper to taste.

For serving, toast buns. Layer chicken and salsa fusion on buns; top with watercress salad and fries.

S.M.O.G. PIE

Serves 8

2 tbsp (30 mL) butter

1 onion, finely chopped

1 cup (250 mL) sliced mushrooms

2 lb (900 g) beef shoulder tenders,
   cut in ½-inch (1 cm) cubes

1½ cups (375 mL) whipping cream

1 cup (250 mL) shredded
   Gruyère cheese

2 tbsp (30 mL) all-purpose flour

Salt and pepper

1 unbaked 9-inch (23 cm)
   double-crust pie shell

Butter, melted, for brushing

Preheat oven to 350°F (180°C).

In a large skillet over medium-high heat, melt 1 tbsp (15 mL) of the butter. Add onion; cook, stirring frequently, until browned. Transfer to a large bowl. In same skillet, melt remaining butter. Add mushrooms; cook until just beginning to soften. Add to onions in bowl. Add beef, cream, and Gruyère to bowl. Sprinkle with flour; mix well. Season with salt and pepper.

Pour mixture into pie shell. Brush edges with water and cover with top crust; crimp edges to seal. Cut a few steam vents in crust and brush with melted butter.

Bake for 50 to 60 minutes or until crust is golden brown and gravy is bubbling through the vents. Let cool 5 to 10 minutes before serving.

When Rodney Henry's music career stopped paying the bills, he started baking the best pies in D.C. to pay for his music habit. That's how he tells it, but the folks of Washington are really happy he pursues both his loves: music and baking dangerously delicious pies.

Though Henry has the classic staples you'd expect to see, like American apple and mixed berry pies, you have to try the S.M.O.G. Pie. That stands for "Steak, Mushroom, Onion, and Gruyère," and it's his most popular pie. Rock on, pie baker, rock on.

HAM HOCK, CHEESE, AND EGG PIE

Serves 10

The classic English pie man has been a thing of rarity if not near extinction on the streets of London, but one man is trying to change that. Chef Andy Bates went from making music videos and commercials to making the best street pies in London. Today, with the help of his mum, the Eat My Pies cart is the hit of Whitecross Market. Bates bakes his sweet and savory creations in his commissary kitchen at the beginning of the day, loads them onto a rickshaw cycle, and sells them all day long.

And indeed, his scrumptious Ham Hock, Cheese, and Egg Pie is perfect any time of day.

1 large ham hock

1 tsp (5 mL) black treacle

Leaves from 1 bunch fresh thyme, chopped

Salt and medium-ground pepper

1 tbsp (15 mL) vegetable oil

1 large onion, chopped

7 oz (200 g) aged Cheddar cheese, shredded

6 tbsp (90 mL) whipping cream

1 lb (450 g) all-purpose flour (3½ cups/875 mL)

¾ cup + 2 tbsp (200 mL) water

¾ cup (175 mL) lard

6 soft-cooked eggs, peeled

Egg wash (1 egg beaten with 1 tsp/2 mL water)

In a large pot, cover ham hock with cold water. Bring to a boil and skim all scum from the surface. Reduce heat to a gentle simmer; add treacle and 1 tsp (5 mL) thyme. Simmer for 2 to 3 hours or until meat is just starting to fall off the bones.

Remove hock from stock. Strain stock into a large saucepan. Bring to a boil; boil until reduced by one-third. Let cool in the pot, then cover and refrigerate until stock is a thick jelly.

Pick meat from hock; trim any visible fat from meat. Flake meat into a bowl; season with pepper and thyme to taste. Add salt if needed (hocks can be very salty). Set aside.

Preheat oven to 350°F (180°C).

In a large skillet, heat oil over medium heat. Add onion; sweat for 5 minutes, until softened but not coloring. Transfer to a medium bowl and let cool. Add Cheddar and cream; mix well. Season with salt and pepper. Set aside.

For the pastry, in a large bowl, stir together flour and a pinch of salt. Make a well in the center. In a saucepan, bring water and lard to a boil; boil until lard is melted. Add to flour and stir with a wooden spoon just to form a smooth dough. Let pastry rest for 5 minutes if it is too hot to handle.

Lightly grease a cake pan with a removable bottom measuring 6 to 8 inches (15 to 20 cm) across and 3 to 4 inches (8 to 10 cm) deep; line bottom with wax paper. Place cake pan on a parchment-lined baking sheet. On a lightly floured work surface, roll out two-thirds of the pastry into a circle large enough to line the cake pan and just hang over the edges. Place pastry into the cake pan, carefully pressing it into the corners. Roll out remaining pastry into a circle just large enough to cover pie.

Cover bottom of pie with ham; top evenly with cheese mixture. Arrange eggs on top. Season eggs with salt and pepper. Brush edges of pastry with egg wash, place top crust on top, and crimp edges to seal. Trim with a knife so no pastry is hanging over the edge. Brush pie with egg wash. Cut a hole in the center.

Bake for 1 hour. Remove sides of pan and brush top and sides of pie with egg wash. Bake for another 15 minutes. Let cool to room temperature, then refrigerate for 2 to 3 hours.

Check pastry for any cracks and holes and fill them with softened butter (so the jelly won't escape). Scrape fat from surface of jelly; gently reheat jelly just until it is liquid. Pour jelly into hole in top crust until pie is filled. Refrigerate pie until jelly is set.

SIZZLING PORK SISIG

Serves 4

Braised Pork

1 pork ear

1 pork jowl

½ pork tongue

½ pork snout

10 cloves garlic

1 cup (250 mL) Filipino soy sauce

½ cup (125 mL) coconut vinegar

3 tbsp (45 mL) salt

4 tsp (20 mL) sugar

1 tsp (5 mL) black peppercorns

Sauté

1 tbsp (15 mL) butter

4 bird's eye chilies, chopped

1 onion, finely chopped

5 cloves garlic, chopped

1 tbsp (15 mL) chopped ginger

¼ cup (60 mL) Filipino soy sauce

2 tbsp (30 mL) coconut vinegar

2 tbsp (30 mL) calamondin (calamansi) juice

4 eggs

Steamed rice for serving

For the braised pork, in a stockpot, combine pork ear, jowl, tongue, snout, garlic, soy sauce, vinegar, salt, sugar, and peppercorns. Add enough water to completely cover pork. Simmer on low heat for 1½ hours or until pork is softened but not completely tender. Remove pork parts from stock and refrigerate to help crisp the skin. Discard stock.

Preheat grill (preferably using mesquite lump charcoal) to high. Grill pork parts, turning, for 20 minutes or until skin is crispy and slightly charred. Refrigerate for about 1 hour.

Preheat 4 fajita platters.

For the sauté, dice pork, discarding any large pieces of fat and any thick cartilage near base of ear. Melt butter in a large skillet over medium-high heat. Sauté chilies, onion, garlic, and ginger for 1 minute. Add pork; sauté for 4 minutes. Stir in soy sauce, vinegar, and calamondin juice; cook for another 2 minutes.

Divide pork mixture among fajita platters. Crack 1 egg onto each platter. Stir egg and pork together. Serve with rice.

When Chef Brian Webb fell in love with Margita, in Phoenix, he had no idea he was about to have a second love affair. When the couple traveled to her hometown in the Philippines to get married, Brian fell for the delicious barbecued pork and chicken coming off the "robata grills" in the streets. While he indulged in as much street food as he could find in the name of "research," people kept calling out to him "Hey Joe!" the local slang for someone of fair complexion.

Brian was so inspired by the flavors that he and Margita opened up the Hey Joe! truck to deliver to the people of Phoenix dishes like this sensational Sizzling Pork Sisig. Don't let words like *jowl* and *snout* freak you out—this is classic Filipino street food, so live a little and try something new!

NOTORIOUS R.I.B.

Serves 10

When you start a food truck, it's important to know your target demographic. The brother-and-sister team at Truck Norris out of Los Angeles knows exactly who loves their fabulous Filipino-Hawaiian fusion the most. These guys take their food seriously, but not much else. As far as they're concerned, life is about three things: food, family, and fun! This outlook plays out in everything from the name of the truck itself to all the menu items.

The Notorious R.I.B. is classic Truck Norris. This one delivers a garlic kick like you've never experienced!

Juice of 1 calamondin (calamansi)
Juice of ½ orange
1 cup (250 mL) soy sauce
¾ cup (175 mL) sugar
½ cup (125 mL) minced garlic
½ cup (125 mL) honey
2 tbsp (30 mL) hot pepper flakes
1 tbsp (15 mL) sesame seeds, toasted
1½ tsp (7 mL) sesame oil
5 lb (2.25 kg) beef short ribs

In a large bowl, stir together calamondin juice, orange juice, soy sauce, sugar, garlic, honey, pepper flakes, sesame seeds, and sesame oil. Add short ribs, turning to coat. Marinate, covered and refrigerated, overnight.

Preheat grill or griddle to medium. Remove ribs from marinade (reserving marinade). Grill ribs, basting frequently with marinade, for 3 to 5 minutes per side, until ribs are coated with a dark glaze. Serve with rice, if desired.

PORK CHOPS WITH LEMON POTATOES

Serves 6

- 1¼ cups (300 mL) extra-virgin olive oil
- Juice of 4 large lemons
- 3 cloves garlic, minced
- 2½ tbsp (37 mL) Greek oregano

- 6 pork chops (about ¾ inch/ 2 cm thick)
- 7 medium unpeeled potatoes, cut in ½-inch (1 cm) wedges
- Salt and pepper
- ¼ cup (60 mL) water

Whisk together ½ cup (125 mL) of the olive oil, half the lemon juice, garlic, and 2 tbsp (30 mL) of the oregano. Put pork chops in a resealable plastic bag, pour in marinade, and marinate, refrigerated, for 6 to 12 hours, turning once or twice.

Preheat oven to 450°F (230°C).

In a large bowl, drizzle about ¼ cup (60 mL) of the olive oil over potatoes. Add remaining 1½ tsp (7 mL) oregano and salt and pepper to taste; toss to coat. Spread potatoes in a single layer in a large shallow baking pan. Pour remaining ½ cup (125 mL) olive oil, remaining lemon juice, and water in between—not over—potatoes. Bake, stirring occasionally, for 45 to 60 minutes, until golden and crispy.

Meanwhile, preheat grill to medium-high. Remove chops from marinade (discarding marinade). Grill chops, turning once, until medium-well done, 10 to 15 minutes. Serve pork chops with potatoes.

At the corner of 51st and Park in New York City you'll find a family-run food truck that brothers Nick and Franky Karagiorgos named after their beloved Uncle Gussy. For over forty years the family has been dishing out the best Greek food on the street, and they have a legion of loyal customers. "Make it nice or make it twice" is their motto, and they treat you like you're eating at their own table.

Nick and Franky happily gave us the recipe for their Pork Chops with Lemon Potatoes, but whatever you do don't tell Uncle Gussy. He'll probably get mad at the guys for giving out recipes to a bunch of *malakas* from a TV show!

PULLED PORK CAESAR SALAD

Serves 4 (with leftover pulled pork)

I think anyone who can work pork into a salad is a genius. In South Carolina, people live for barbecue, but there weren't many trucks doing it well in Columbia, so Chef Scott Hall opened up Bone-In Artisan Barbecue. Aptly named, because he cooks the pork shoulders with the bone still in.

The Pulled Pork Caesar Salad is a masterpiece and maybe the most memorable salad experience you will have, guaranteed. This one hits you with so many flavors you won't know where it's coming from.

Pulled Pork

1½ cups (375 mL) kosher salt
¾ cup (175 mL) molasses
8 cups (2 L) water
1 boneless pork shoulder (4 lb/1.8 kg)
1 tsp (5 mL) cumin seeds
1 tsp (5 mL) fennel seeds
1 tsp (5 mL) coriander seeds
1 tbsp (15 mL) chili powder
1 tbsp (15 mL) onion powder
1 tbsp (15 mL) paprika

Caesar Vinaigrette

¼ cup (60 mL) garlic, minced
1 tbsp (15 mL) anchovy paste
3 egg yolks
3 tbsp (45 mL) Dijon mustard
4 tsp (20 mL) lemon juice
4 tsp (20 mL) cider vinegar

½ cup (125 mL) grated Parmigiano-Reggiano cheese
¾ cup (175 mL) extra-virgin olive oil
3 tbsp (45 mL) water
1½ tsp (7 mL) pepper

Croutons

1 tsp (5 mL) ground cumin
1 tsp (5 mL) garlic powder
1 tsp (5 mL) smoked paprika
1 tsp (5 mL) kosher salt
2 cups (500 mL) 1½-inch (4 cm) cubes cornbread or other bread

Salad

2 tbsp (30 mL) butter
1 tbsp (15 mL) anchovy paste
3 cloves garlic, finely chopped
2 heads baby romaine lettuce
3 oz (85 g) Parmigiano-Reggiano cheese

Begin the pulled pork 1 or 2 days ahead. In a large pot, combine salt, molasses, and water. Add pork shoulder; add more water if necessary to cover pork. Cover and refrigerate for 8 to 12 hours (the longer, the better). In a spice grinder, finely grind cumin, fennel, and coriander seeds. Transfer to a small bowl and stir in chili powder, onion powder, and paprika. Set dry rub aside.

Prepare grill or smoker with wood chips of your choice; preheat grill on high until chips smoke vigorously, about 20 minutes. Lower heat to medium. Remove pork from brine and pat dry. Sift dry rub evenly over pork. Wearing rubber gloves (to help dry rub stick), pat dry rub onto meat so it adheres. Place pork on greased grill over drip pan. Close lid and smoke pork at 210°F (100°C), adding more wood chips if necessary,

for 14 hours or until pork pulls apart easily with a fork. (If using a conventional oven, preheat to 210°F/100°C and cook pork, uncovered, for 14 hours.) Remove pork from smoker and let rest for at least 1 hour. Pull half the meat apart with two forks; set aside. (Keep remaining pork, covered and refrigerated, for another use.)

For the Caesar vinaigrette, in a blender, purée garlic with anchovy paste, scraping down sides once or twice. Add egg yolks, mustard, lemon juice, vinegar, and Parmesan. Blend until well combined. With the motor running, add olive oil in a steady stream until just incorporated. Transfer dressing to a small bowl; stir in water and pepper. Refrigerate if not using immediately.

In a large bowl, stir together reserved pulled pork and 2 cups (500 mL) of the Caesar vinaigrette. Marinate, covered and refrigerated, for at least 2 hours or overnight.

For the croutons, preheat oven to 350°F (180°C). Stir together cumin, garlic powder, paprika, and salt. Spread bread cubes in a single layer on a baking sheet. Coat bread lightly with cooking spray (or toss with a few spoonfuls of oil); season all over with spice mix. Bake croutons, turning once, until golden brown, about 10 minutes.

For the salad, preheat grill to medium-high. In a small saucepan over medium-high heat, melt butter. Add anchovy paste and garlic. Simmer, stirring occasionally, for 5 minutes (do not let garlic burn). Remove from heat.

Cut each romaine in half lengthwise. Brush cut sides with anchovy-garlic butter. Grill romaine, buttered side down, until grill marks appear and lettuce is slightly wilted, about 2 minutes. (Romaine can also be seared in a large skillet over medium-high heat.) Transfer romaine, cut side up, to 4 plates. Drizzle each half with remaining Caesar vinaigrette. Top with marinated pulled pork. Serve garnished with spiced croutons and shaved Parmesan.

SHASHLIK WITH TZATZIKI

Serves 8

Shashlik

2 large onions

1 boneless New Zealand or Australian leg of lamb (3½ to 4 lb/1.5 to 1.8 kg), trimmed of fat

Chopped fresh mint and rosemary

Salt

2 lemons, halved

Tzatziki

2 cups (500 mL) Greek-style plain yogurt

10 cloves garlic, minced

1 to 2 cucumbers, shredded

Chopped fresh dill

Sugar (optional)

Begin the shashlik 1 to 3 days ahead. In a food processor, purée onions; transfer to a large bowl. Cut lamb into 1-inch (2.5 cm) chunks with a minimum of fat; add to bowl with onions. Add mint, rosemary, and salt to taste. Mix well to coat lamb thoroughly. Marinate, covered and refrigerated, for 1 to 3 days.

For the tzatziki, in a bowl, stir together yogurt and garlic. Stir in shredded cucumber and dill to taste. Stir in sugar, if desired, to cut the sharpness of the garlic. Refrigerate, covered, until needed.

Preheat grill to high; soak bamboo skewers in water for at least 30 minutes. Thread lamb onto skewers. (Skewers can be prepared ahead of time and refrigerated.) Sprinkle lamb with salt; grill, turning frequently, until medium-rare, 7 to 12 minutes. Transfer to a platter and squirt with lemon juice. Serve with tzatziki and rice, if desired.

Jamaican-Uzbeki fusion ... I think that says it all, really. Chef Ed Cornelia does barbecue so well that the Boston lunch crowd adjust their schedules to have the time to wait for his amazing sandwiches and signature shashliks. *Shashlik* is the Russian word for skewered meat, and nobody is doing it better than Silk Road BBQ.

Cornelia cooks his meats to perfection over hardwood charcoal. Some dishes can take up to eight minutes to prepare. That doesn't *sound* like much, but to a food cart on a busy lunch schedule, that "ticket time" is forever. But according to the workers in the surrounding office towers, it's worth the wait. The delicious smell of Ed's blend of spices wafting from the barbecue makes work impossible anyway!

LAMB SAUSAGE AND ARUGULA SALAD

Serves 4 (with leftover sausage)

Ben Ackerman and Jesse Allen got tired of working in other people's kitchens, but they still loved cooking. In fact they love creating delicious dishes so much, they both have "mise en place" tattooed on their forearms. (That's kitchen terminology for "everything in place," and it's important when you work in a ten-by-five trailer!) Harnessing their knowledge of local markets, their culinary skills, and their entrepreneurial spirit, they roll on the streets of Lansing, Michigan, in Trailer Park'd. In their words, "We do what we want and we basically smoke a lot of meat."

Ben and Jesse say you have to promise you'll make your own lamb sausage from scratch...don't let them down!

Lamb Sausage

2½ lb (1.125 kg) boneless leg of lamb, cubed and chilled

½ lb (225 g) lamb fat, cubed and frozen

¼ cup (60 mL) red wine vinegar

2 tbsp (30 mL) minced garlic

2 tsp (10 mL) minced fresh sage

4 tsp (20 mL) kosher salt

2 tsp (10 mL) pepper

1½ tsp (7 mL) ground toasted fennel seeds

Salad

3 to 4 corncobs, husked

1 lb (450 g) lamb sausages

6 oz (170 g) organic arugula

4 tsp (20 mL) olive oil

Kosher salt

½ cup (125 mL) pickled sweet peppers

¼ cup (60 mL) shredded Asiago cheese

¼ cup (60 mL) honey

Pepper

For the sausage, combine lamb and lamb fat; mix well. Grind meat through a chilled meat grinder fitted with the coarse plate into a chilled large bowl. Add vinegar, garlic, sage, salt, pepper, and fennel; mix well. Pipe into sausage casings (you will need about 8 feet/2.5 m of casings). (Alternatively, shape sausage mixture into patties.)

For the salad, grill or broil corn, turning frequently, until crisp and golden brown. Slice kernels from cobs. You should have ¾ cup (175 mL) kernels. Set aside.

Grill sausages (or fry patties in a large skillet over medium-high heat) until nicely browned and a meat thermometer reads 145°F (65°C). Thickly slice sausages (or break patties into bite-size chunks).

In a bowl, toss arugula with olive oil and salt to taste; divide among 4 plates. Scatter corn and sausage over top, then dress salad with pickled sweet peppers. Sprinkle with Asiago, drizzle with honey, and finish with a grind of pepper.

THAI STIR-FRY

Serves 2

Fistful of flat wide rice noodles

1 tsp (5 mL) vegetable oil

1 tsp (5 mL) minced garlic

2 Thai chilies, seeded if desired, thinly sliced

6 oz (170 g) chicken, pork, or tofu, cut into strips, or peeled shrimp

½ cup (125 mL) chopped onion

1 tbsp (15 mL) dark soy sauce

1½ tsp (7 mL) fish sauce

½ tsp (2 mL) sugar

1 large tomato, chopped

½ cup (125 mL) thinly sliced sweet red pepper

½ cup (125 mL) thinly sliced sweet green pepper

1 tbsp (15 mL) thinly sliced fresh basil

Soak noodles in hot water until soft and transparent; drain. Heat oil in a wok over high heat. Add garlic and chilies; stir-fry for 1 minute. Add chicken; stir-fry until browned. Add noodles, onion, soy sauce, fish sauce, and sugar; stir-fry for 2 minutes. Add tomato, red and green peppers, and basil; stir-fry for 1 minute.

On the North Shore of Oahu, a food truck challenged the incredible surf for the title of "Most Famous Thing on the Island." Opal's Thai food truck was a gem. Chef Opal grew up in Thailand, and his dishes are 100 percent authentic. Most of his ingredients, such as mangoes, limes, coconuts, and green papayas, were grown right down the road from the truck. Where most city trucks are concerned with speed and volume, Chef Opal took the time to ask everyone questions and then customized their orders. He wanted every dish he made to deliver the best experience.

This stir-fry is a perfect example of what you'd find at his truck (or now find at his restaurant). Every bite has a little bit of his ingredients but a lot of his philosophy.

SWEET WHEELS

Good things come to those who wait, so let's get to the sweet wheels!

In our travels we came across quite a few specialty dessert trucks serving up only the sugary treats, so we were quite surprised when more than a few of the recipes in this chapter came from hard-core barbecue or seafood wagons. I should have figured this out by now, but you really can't judge a truck by its wrapping.

Here you will find your fair share of cakes, brownies, and cookies, but not everything is calorie-laden. In fact, one of the recipes might just be the healthiest in the entire book!

People who run food trucks tend to be very experimental and . . . well, playful with their food. These sweet recipes are by far the most creative and unexpected. But whether savory, sweet, or just plain weird, we're quite sure they will all bring a smile to your face.

It just goes to prove that the food truck revolution has something for everyone!

SWEET WHEELS

APPLE PIE "KOOL-AID"

Serves 4

Ian Kleinman can easily claim the title of having the only liquid-nitrogen ice-cream truck on the streets of Denver—or maybe anywhere. Using liquid nitrogen to "cook" his creations, Ian has mastered some pretty cool techniques. Normal ice cream takes about eight minutes to make, but Ian can do it in forty-five seconds! Fryer oil is heated to around 350°F; liquid nitrogen is 320°—at the other end of the scale!

Not too many people have liquid nitrogen in the pantry, so Ian gave us the recipe for his fabulous Apple Pie "Kool-aid." It's just as much fun to make and enjoy, without any chance of a really extreme ice-cream headache!

Green Apple Syrup

2 green apples, unpeeled
1¼ cups (300 mL) sugar
1 cup (250 mL) water

Pie Crust

6 tbsp (90 mL) all-purpose flour
4 tbsp (60 mL) butter, chilled and cubed

2 tbsp (30 mL) sugar
1 tsp (5 mL) cinnamon
2 tbsp (30 mL) cold water

Kool-aid

8 cups (2 L) filtered water
¾ cup (175 mL) green apple syrup

Make the green apple syrup the day before. Cut apple flesh away from core. Place apples in a large saucepan; add sugar and water. Bring to a boil over high heat; boil for 25 minutes. Strain apples, discarding solids. Refrigerate syrup overnight. Set aside 2 tbsp (30 mL) of the syrup for rimming glasses.

For the pie crust, preheat oven to 350°F (180°C). In a small bowl, combine flour and butter; cut in butter with a fork until pea-size pieces of butter have formed. Stir in sugar and cinnamon. Stir in water until mixture just comes together. Spread mixture on a baking sheet. Bake for 20 minutes or until golden brown. Let cool. In a coffee grinder or mini food processor, process crust mixture to a fine powder.

For the kool-aid, in a large jug, combine water and green apple syrup. Refrigerate.

For each serving, dip the rim of a glass into reserved apple syrup. Roll rim in pie crust crumbs. Fill glass with ice and add the kool-aid. (Leftover syrup keeps, refrigerated, for 1 week.)

THE JUICE TRUCK | *Vancouver, British Columbia*

STRAWBERRY COCONUT SMOOTHIE

Serves 4

- 1½ frozen bananas
- 3 Medjool dates
- 2 cups (500 mL) fresh strawberries
- 2 cups (500 mL) coconut milk
- ½ cup (125 mL) coconut water
- 2 tbsp (30 mL) cacao nibs
- ⅛ tsp (0.5 mL) ground vanilla

In a blender, combine bananas, dates, strawberries, coconut milk, coconut water, cacao nibs, and vanilla; blend until smooth.

Ryan Slater and Zach Berman consider their truck the perfect blend of an experimental laboratory and an artists' studio. They fell in love with exotic juices and blends on their world travels and thought the perfect place to experiment with—and sell—their juices was the streets of Vancouver.

They pack more vitamins into a single serving of juice than most North Americans get in a full meal. This smoothie is one of the simplest recipes in the entire book, but wow, does it pack a refreshing punch!

ORANGE CREAM DREAM CUPCAKES

Makes 12 cupcakes

Cupcakes

¼ cup (60 mL) butter, softened

1 cup (250 mL) sugar

1 egg

1 tsp (5 mL) orange food color (optional)

1 tsp (5 mL) pure orange extract

¼ tsp (1 mL) pure vanilla extract

½ tsp (2 mL) baking powder

¼ tsp (1 mL) baking soda

¼ tsp (1 mL) salt

1⅓ cups (325 mL) all-purpose flour

1 cup (250 mL) buttermilk

Filling

½ cup (125 mL) butter, at room temperature

1 cup (250 mL) icing sugar

Pinch of salt

1 cup (250 mL) marshmallow fluff

1¼ tsp (6 mL) pure vanilla extract

Frosting

5 tbsp (75 mL) butter

1½ tsp (7 mL) pure orange extract

3 cups (750 mL) icing sugar

½ cup (125 mL) whipping cream

¼ tsp (1 mL) orange food color (optional)

For the cupcakes, preheat oven to 350°F (180°C). Line a 12-cup muffin pan with paper liners.

In the bowl of a stand mixer fitted with the paddle attachment, beat butter with sugar until light and fluffy. Beating continuously, add egg, food color (if using), orange extract, vanilla extract, baking powder, baking soda, and salt. With mixer on low speed, alternately stir in flour and milk, in three additions. Scrape down sides of bowl as needed. Divide batter evenly among cupcake liners.

Bake for 18 to 20 minutes or until a toothpick inserted into a cupcake comes out clean. Cool completely on a rack before removing cupcakes from pan.

For the filling, using an electric mixer, beat butter until fluffy. With mixer on low speed, add icing sugar and salt; mix well. Beat in marshmallow fluff and vanilla. Transfer filling to a pastry bag. Using a ¼-inch (5 mm) round tip, insert the tip a little more than halfway into a cupcake. While pushing the filling into the cupcake, pull the tip out of the cupcake.

For the frosting, using an electric mixer, cream butter until smooth. Beat in orange extract. With mixer on low speed, gradually add icing sugar. Scrape sides of bowl as needed. Add cream and orange food color (if using); beat on high speed until frosting is light and fluffy. Frost the cupcakes.

If you ask Orlando's Alex Marin and Joey Conicella what the single most important ingredient is in their cupcakes, they will answer without hesitation: "Love!" Their cute little cakes are an uncomplicated throwback to the days when Grandma would whip up something simply delicious.

These are called Orange Cream Dreams because that's what you will be thinking about in your sleep!

MAPLE BACON CUPCAKES

Makes 12 cupcakes

The brother-sister team of Stephanie and Danny Diaz had one of the first dessert-only trucks on the streets of Miami, and they still have the best-smelling truck on the road. But what do you expect from a truck that specializes in deep-frying cupcakes! Their mom taught them everything they know, and apparently their mom knew a lot about how to make sugar come to life.

The Maple Bacon Cupcakes are bestsellers, as you would expect with any menu item combining the sweet and savory flavors of these two powerhouse ingredients.

Cupcakes

4 cups (1 L) maple syrup

5 slices applewood-smoked bacon

2¾ cups (650 mL) cake-and-pastry flour, sifted

1 tbsp (15 mL) baking powder

3 eggs, at room temperature

½ cup (125 mL) vegetable oil

1 cup (250 mL) milk

1 tsp (5 mL) pure maple extract

Icing and finishing

6 tbsp (90 mL) butter, softened

4 cups (1 L) icing sugar

¼ cup (60 mL) maple syrup

2 tsp (10 mL) pure maple extract

Coarse sea salt for garnish

In a medium saucepan, boil maple syrup until reduced to 2 cups (500 mL). Set aside.

In a skillet, fry bacon until browned but not completely crisp. Drain on paper towels. Chop. Set aside 12 pieces for garnish; set aside remaining bacon.

Preheat oven to 350°F (180°C). Line a 12-cup muffin pan with paper liners.

Sift together flour and baking powder. In a large bowl, beat eggs until light and fluffy. Slowly add oil and reduced maple syrup, beating until combined. Add flour mixture; beat well until combined. Add milk and maple extract; beat until combined. Fold in chopped bacon. Divide batter evenly among cupcake liners, filling each three-quarters full.

Bake until golden and a toothpick inserted into the center comes out clean, about 20 minutes. Cool completely on a rack before removing cupcakes from pan.

For the icing, in a large bowl, beat butter until light and fluffy. Beat in icing sugar 1 cup (250 mL) at a time until fully incorporated. Add maple syrup and maple extract; beat until combined and fluffy.

Frost the cupcakes, sprinkle with sea salt, and garnish with a piece of bacon.

DIABLO'S DELIGHTS

Makes 12 doughnuts

4 slices thick-cut bacon

4 cups (1 L) soybean oil

1 or 2 cans refrigerated biscuit dough (enough for 12 biscuits)

1 can (12 oz/340 g) cream cheese frosting

¼ cup (60 mL) jalapeño jam

Cook bacon until browned but not crisp. Drain on paper towels. Let cool. Chop into small pieces. Set aside.

In a deep-fryer or deep, heavy saucepan, heat oil to 375°F (190°C). Meanwhile, on a lightly floured work surface, separate dough into 12 biscuits; pat biscuits into 2-inch (5 cm) circles. (If using flat biscuit dough, roll out dough to about ½ inch/1 cm thickness; cut out circles with a cookie cutter.) Using a plastic bottle cap or 1-inch (2.5 cm) cookie cutter, cut circles from middle of biscuits. Working in batches if necessary, carefully set doughnuts into hot oil. Cook on one side for 20 to 30 seconds, then flip and cook until golden brown, another 20 to 30 seconds. Using a skimmer, remove doughnuts and drain on paper towels.

Place cream cheese frosting in a squeeze bottle (or place in a resealable plastic bag, then cut off one corner). Squirt a generous dollop onto middle of each doughnut. Spoon 1 tsp (5 mL) jalapeño jam onto frosting. Top with bacon bits.

It is impossible to say which is sweeter, Jasmine Listou or her Denver trailer, Sugar Lips. Raised on health food for most of her life, Jasmine rebelled by converting a 1961 Cardinal trailer (complete with pink flamingos and gnomes) into the finest four-wheeled fryer in the Mountain Time Zone.

Along with her other hits, like Smores doughnuts, Diablo's Delights are made fresh right in front of your eyes and contain a lot of stuff you wouldn't expect to see on a doughnut. Bacon, cream cheese frosting, and jalapeño jam? Who knows temptation more than el diablo himself? Once you give these a try, you'll see what we mean by devilishly good!

CHEWY CARAMEL BROWNIES

Makes 9 to 12 brownies

Brownies

¾ cup (175 mL) unsalted butter (1½ sticks)

3 oz (85 g) unsweetened chocolate, chopped

2 oz (55 g) bittersweet chocolate, chopped

2 eggs

1½ tsp (7 mL) pure vanilla extract

1¼ cups (300 mL) sugar

¾ cup (175 mL) all-purpose flour

1 tbsp (15 mL) cocoa powder

½ cup (125 mL) semisweet chocolate chips (optional)

½ cup (125 mL) chopped pecans or walnuts (optional)

Chocolate Ganache

¾ cup (175 mL) whipping cream

2 cups (500 mL) semisweet chocolate chips or chopped chocolate (12 oz/340 g)

Caramel Topping

½ cup (125 mL) soft caramel candies

¼ cup (60 mL) whipping cream

Forget "Power to the people." At the Treats Truck in Brooklyn, the motto is "Sugar to the people!" Owner Kim Ima wanted to bring homemade baked goods and treats to the streets, and she rolls in her truck, aptly named Sugar. Kim loves chocolate so much that if she could, I bet she would fill the gas tank with it.

Among many other creative uses of flour and sugar, her chewy Caramel Brownies will make you fanatical about the power of sugar as well.

For the brownies, preheat oven to 350°F (180°C). Grease a 9-inch (2.5 L) square cake pan (or line pan with foil and grease the foil). If doubling the batch, use a 13- × 9-inch (3.5 L) pan.

Melt butter, unsweetened chocolate, and bittersweet chocolate in a medium saucepan over low heat, stirring until melted and smooth (or use a microwave). Watch carefully to prevent burning. Remove from heat. Meanwhile, in a small bowl, lightly beat eggs with vanilla. Stir sugar into melted chocolate, then stir in eggs. Add flour and cocoa powder; stir or whisk until just combined—do not overmix. Spread in prepared pan. If you're using chocolate chips or nuts, mix them into the batter first and/or sprinkle them on top of the batter before baking, pressing them down a bit into the batter. Bake for 30 to 35 minutes or until a knife or toothpick inserted in the center comes out almost clean. Let brownies cool completely before lifting them from the pan.

For the ganache, in a small saucepan, heat cream to just before a boil. Reduce heat to low and add chocolate, stirring until melted and smooth. (Or microwave cream and chocolate, stirring every 15 seconds, until melted and smooth.) Ganache can be made a little thicker or thinner as needed by adding a bit more chocolate or cream. Let stand until spreadable, about 30 minutes. Spread ganache over cooled brownies.

For the caramel topping, in the top of a double boiler over simmering water (or in a saucepan over low heat), melt caramels with cream, stirring until melted and smooth. (Or microwave cream and caramels for 30 seconds, then stir; continue to microwave, stirring every 15 seconds, until melted and smooth.) Add more caramels as needed to make topping thicker if desired (or add more cream for a thinner topping). Drizzle caramel over ganache; swirl it into ganache if desired. Cut into squares.

CHOCOLATE DIABLO COOKIES

Makes 12 big (or more small) cookies

1½ cups (375 mL) sifted
    all-purpose flour

1 cup (250 mL) sifted cocoa powder

1 tsp (5 mL) baking soda

1 tsp (5 mL) cinnamon

1 tsp (5 mL) cayenne pepper
    (or more if you like it hot!)

1 cup (250 mL) chocolate
    chips or chunks

2 eggs

1 cup (250 mL) brown sugar

1 cup (250 mL) granulated sugar

½ cup (125 mL) canola oil

3 tbsp (45 mL) freshly squeezed
    ginger juice or grated fresh ginger

1 tbsp (15 mL) pure vanilla extract

Coarse salt and granulated
    sugar for sprinkling

Preheat oven to 375°F (190°C). Grease a baking sheet.

In a large bowl, sift together flour, cocoa powder, baking soda, cinnamon, and cayenne. Stir in chocolate. In a medium bowl, lightly beat eggs. Add brown sugar, granulated sugar, oil, ginger juice, and vanilla; whisk until well blended. Add to dry ingredients; stir until combined.

Divide batter into 12 fist-size balls (or smaller balls, if desired). Arrange on baking sheet and press to flatten slightly (cookies will spread quite a lot while baking). Sprinkle with coarse salt and sugar.

Bake for 11 minutes or until cookies start to crack. They should still be fudgy in the middle. Cool on racks.

Of all the amazing things that come out of Tacofino's window in Tofino, B.C., even we didn't expect one of the best dessert items of all time. Wife and husband Kaeli Robinsong and Jason Sussman are master chefs whose focus on fresh gourmet ingredients makes theirs one of the best taco trucks in North America.

But wow, you gotta try their Chocolate Diablo Cookies! How many times have you said, "Come on over and try my spicy chocolate chili ginger cookie"? Exactly what I thought… never. Until *now!* In Tofino the surf may be up, but sit this one out, 'cause it's time for milk and cookies.

MISSION ST. FRENCH TOAST

Serves 4

4 prickly pears (or 1½ cups/375 mL
   prickly pear purée)

2 cups (500 mL) halved strawberries

¼ cup + 2 tsp (60 mL + 10 mL) sugar

1 cup (250 mL) whipping cream

6 eggs

4 bolillos or thick slices
   white bread

½ cup (125 mL) butter, melted

Maple syrup for serving

Remove skin from prickly pears, carefully avoiding thorns. Coarsely chop prickly pears; transfer to a medium saucepan. Bring to simmer and cook for 5 minutes, stirring occasionally. Remove from heat and let cool slightly. Press through a fine-mesh sieve set over a bowl; discard solids.

In same saucepan, combine prickly pear juice, strawberries, and ¼ cup (60 mL) of the sugar. Cook over medium heat, stirring frequently to prevent burning, for 20 minutes or until mixture is reduced and has thickened. Let cool to room temperature. (*Jam keeps, refrigerated, for up to 3 days.*)

In a large bowl, beat cream until it begins to thicken slightly. Add the remaining 2 tsp (10 mL) sugar. Beat cream to medium stiffness, or until it holds its shape when whisk is lifted.

In a medium bowl, beat eggs with 3 tbsp (45 mL) of the whipped cream.

Heat a griddle or large nonstick skillet over medium heat. Slice each bolillo diagonally into 4 pieces. Dip bread in egg batter, letting soak for 30 seconds. Brush griddle with a hearty amount of melted butter. Cook French toast for 2 minutes per side or until golden brown and heated through. Serve topped with prickly pear jam, whipped cream, and maple syrup.

People in San Francisco have a different way of going about things, and when it comes to French toast, it couldn't be any more avant-garde or delicious! The Fogcutter is a classic "torta," or street sandwich, truck combining every style of cooking known to mankind, from Vietnamese to Italian to Mexican. And when the focus turns to French toast, it's the reigning champ.

I don't know if it's the prickly pear jam or the strawberries or the maple syrup, but this is a taste combination that you just have to try! Some people leave their hearts in San Francisco, but not me… I left my hunger.

HAWAIIAN FRENCH TOAST

Serves 3

If breakfast is the most important meal of the day, then you are going to love this recipe. Gigi Pascual is a pastry arts major who found that the comfort foods her clients loved the most were breakfasts, which was fine with her because that was her favorite meal of the day, too!

At L.A.'s Buttermilk Truck, Pascual offers both sweet and savory creations that blur the lines and make you wonder if it's lunchtime, brunch time, dinner, or dessert. It really doesn't matter, because it's all so good. For example, this Hawaiian French Toast makes a perfect dessert… or breakfast, or lunch. Whatever—go crazy!

Hawaiian Bread

1½ tsp (7 mL) active dry yeast

3 tbsp (45 mL) warm water (115°F/45°C)

1 egg

⅓ cup (75 mL) pineapple juice

3 tbsp (45 mL) room-temperature water

3 tbsp (45 mL) butter, melted

½ tsp (2 mL) pure vanilla extract

¼ cup (60 mL) sugar

Pinch of ground ginger

2 cups (500 mL) all-purpose flour

French Toast

3 eggs

1 cup (250 mL) milk

2 tsp (10 mL) cinnamon

1 tsp (5 mL) pure vanilla extract

½ tsp (2 mL) baking powder

Pinch of nutmeg

Pinch of salt

Flour for dredging

2 tbsp (30 mL) butter

For the Hawaiian bread, in a small bowl, dissolve yeast in warm water. Let stand until creamy, about 10 minutes.

In a large bowl, combine yeast mixture, egg, pineapple juice, room-temperature water, butter, vanilla, sugar, and ginger; beat until well mixed. Gradually stir in flour until a stiff batter is formed. Cover with a damp cloth and let rise in a warm place for 1 hour.

Lightly grease an 8- or 9-inch (1.2 or 1.5 L) round cake pan. Deflate dough and turn it out onto a well-floured work surface. Shape into a round loaf. Place dough in cake pan. Cover with a damp cloth and let rise until doubled in volume, about 40 minutes.

Meanwhile, preheat oven to 350°F (180°C).

Bake bread for 25 to 30 minutes or until bottom sounds hollow when tapped. Cool on a rack.

For the French toast, slice bread and dry on a rack for at least 2 hours or overnight. In a medium bowl, beat eggs. Whisk in milk, cinnamon, vanilla, baking powder, nutmeg, and salt. Put flour for dredging in a shallow dish. In a large skillet over medium-high heat, melt butter. Dip each bread slice into egg mixture until well soaked, then dredge in flour. Cook bread, in batches, for about 2 minutes per side or until golden brown and crisp. Serve with maple syrup.

STICKY NANAS

Serves 4

2 cups (500 mL) vegetable oil	4 or 5 potsticker wrappers
1 banana	1 egg
4 tsp (20 mL) brown sugar	½ cup (125 mL) water

In a deep, wide skillet, heat oil over medium-high heat.

Peel banana and cut into small chunks. In a bowl, toss banana with brown sugar. Place a spoonful of banana filling in the center of each potsticker wrapper.

Beat together egg and water. Brush egg wash around edge of half of each potsticker wrapper. Fold over other half and press edges together to seal.

Fry until golden. Drain on paper towels; let cool. Serve drizzled with white chocolate and caramel sauces and dusted with icing sugar, if desired.

In Las Vegas, Asian fusion isn't hard to find. But wow! The guys at Tasty Bunz are doing it really well! Owner Ej Estrella's menu is based on Asian bao buns, which are usually filled with meats or vegetables. But whether he knows it or not, he makes one of the best desserts on four wheels.

Sticky Nanas are addictive potstickers filled with bananas and brown sugar, a spin on a classic Filipino dessert that has the Vegas fans doubling down to get some.

ZEPPOLE

Serves 4

For all its size, Los Angeles has a Chinatown and a Koreatown, but no Little Italy. That was, until Rosa and her brother Rico rolled out Rosa's Bella Cucina, the most Italian truck in the city. And you know they're serious about their cooking when they fly in prosciutto direct from Italy.

Zeppole are delicious deep-fried doughnuts coated in powdered sugar, and Rosa's were so popular they couldn't keep up with demand. So Rosa's house-building father showed her how to mix a big batch of batter—with a power drill and a cement mixer! This recipe is scaled down a bit, so you won't have to do it that way—but how much fun would it be if you did?!

1 pkg active dry yeast
⅛ tsp (0.5 mL) salt
⅛ tsp (0.5 mL) sugar
1 cup (250 mL) warm water

2 eggs, lightly beaten
1¼ cups (300 mL) all-purpose flour
1½ cups (375 mL) corn oil
Icing sugar

In a large bowl, whisk yeast, salt, and sugar into water. Stir in eggs and flour, blending well. Cover and let rise in a warm area for 90 minutes or until bubbly and doubled in size.

In a small skillet or sauté pan, heat oil to 375°F (190°C). Working in batches of 4, drop level tablespoons of dough into oil. Fry for 2 minutes per side or until golden brown. Drain well on paper towels; sprinkle with icing sugar while hot. Serve warm.

CARROT CAKE PIEROGIES

Serves 8

Pierogi Dough

4 cups (1 L) all-purpose flour

1 tbsp (15 mL) salt

1¼ cups (300 mL) cold water

1 tbsp (15 mL) canola oil

Carrot Cake Filling

1 sweet potato, peeled and
  coarsely chopped

3 cups (750 mL) coarsely
  chopped carrots

½ cup (125 mL) raisins

1 tbsp (15 mL) canola oil

1 cup (250 mL) cream cheese

½ cup (125 mL) brown sugar

½ cup (125 mL) granulated sugar

1 tbsp (15 mL) cinnamon

1 tbsp (15 mL) ground allspice

Caramel Sauce

½ cup (125 mL) butter

2 cups (500 mL) sugar

3 cups (750 mL) whipping cream,
  at room temperature

Pinch of cinnamon

Mint Oil

4 cups (1 L) olive oil

1 cup (250 mL) fresh mint leaves

For finishing

2 tbsp (30 mL) butter

Icing sugar

The best thing about a pierogi is that you can pretty much jam anything in there, boil it up, and it'll taste great. They're little pockets of goodness that just keep on giving! And in Calgary, nobody does them better than Curtis Berry and Brendan Bankowski. They're doing everything from the traditional onion-and-sauerkraut you'd find in your Babcia's pot right through to their Mexi-cali Perogy, with flavors inspired by a taco.

Being of Polish descent myself, my favorite has always been a good dessert pierogi. In fact, these are outstanding. Even *my* Babcia would love them!

For the pierogi dough, in a large bowl, stir together flour, salt, water, and oil until a soft but not sticky dough forms. Knead on a lightly floured surface, adding more water or flour as needed, until dough is smooth. Cover with plastic wrap and let rest for about 20 minutes.

For the filling, in a food processor, combine sweet potato, carrots, and raisins; pulse until finely chopped. Heat oil in a large skillet over medium heat. Add carrot mixture; cook, stirring, until just softened. Transfer to a bowl. Add cream cheese, brown sugar, granulated sugar, cinnamon, and allspice; stir until well combined. Set aside.

For the caramel sauce, in a medium saucepan over medium-high heat, melt butter. Add sugar; cook, stirring constantly to avoid burning, until caramel is golden brown. Add cream and cinnamon; whisk until smooth. Set aside, keeping warm.

For the mint oil, heat oil in a medium saucepan over low heat. Add mint. Simmer on low heat for 10 minutes. Strain, discarding mint. Set oil aside.

To finish the pierogies, on a lightly floured work surface, roll out dough
to ¼-inch (5 mm) thickness. Cut out 3-inch (8 cm) rounds with a glass or
cookie cutter. Place 1 tbsp (15 mL) filling on each round. Fold dough over
and pinch edges together to seal.

Bring a large pot of salted water to a boil. Cook pierogies, stirring gently,
until they float, 1 or 2 minutes. Transfer to a colander to drain.

In a large skillet over medium-high heat, melt butter. Add pierogies;
fry until golden brown on both sides. Divide pierogies among plates.
Drizzle with caramel sauce, sprinkle with icing sugar, and garnish
with a splash of mint oil.

SPICY APPLE BOTTOMS CRÊPES

Serves 7

4 eggs

2 cups (500 mL) skim milk

1½ cups (375 mL) all-purpose flour

¼ cup (60 mL) canola oil

2 tbsp (30 mL) cinnamon sugar

4 Fuji apples, thinly sliced

1 tsp (5 mL) cinnamon

½ cup (125 mL) caramel sauce

¼ cup (60 mL) icing sugar

Whipped cream for serving

In a blender, combine eggs, milk, flour, oil, and cinnamon sugar; blend on high until no lumps remain. Set aside.

Preheat oven to 200°F (100°C).

Spread apple slices in a large skillet over medium-high heat. Sprinkle with cinnamon. Cook apples, turning occasionally, until soft, about 5 minutes. Set aside.

Heat a medium nonstick skillet over medium-high heat; coat lightly with canola oil. Pour ½ cup (125 mL) batter into pan while swirling pan so batter coats the bottom. Cook for 30 seconds. Using a spatula to loosen the edges, flip crêpe. Spread a large spoonful of cinnamon apples down center of crêpe; cook for 30 seconds. Fold sides of crêpe over apples. Roll or slide crêpe onto a plate with the folded side down. Keep warm in oven while you repeat with remaining batter and apples.

Serve crêpes topped with caramel sauce, icing sugar, and whipped cream.

I met the best dessert in California at a truck with a moustache named Gaston. Married couple Christian and Danielle Murcia wanted to bring the crêpes they had enjoyed in the streets of Paris back to their home in Orange County— and they have succeeded.

The Spicy Apple Bottoms is the perfect way to end the day or any meal. It is filled with sweet, cinnamony apples and topped with caramel sauce and whipped cream. I guarantee you will need a nap— if not some insulin!

STRAWBERRY AND NUTELLA CRÊPES

Serves 8

Baton Rouge, Louisiana. You would think that with its rich French tradition and history, good crêpes would be easy to find. But Chef Kevin Black discovered otherwise. Taking up the charge, he launched GOyaya's Crepes and traveled all over town making sure no one was ever far from a delicious French wrap. So successful was his truck, he had to plant roots, and since we featured him on the show he's moved into a bricks-and-mortar home—and his crêpes are as popular as ever.

This Strawberry and Nutella Crêpe is perfect for dessert. Don't let the mystique of crêpes intimidate you—I can attest that it doesn't take much to pull one off.

4 eggs
1 cup (250 mL) milk
1 cup (250 mL) water
¼ cup (60 mL) butter, melted
1½ cups (375 mL) all-purpose flour
Pinch of salt
Nutella
Sliced fresh strawberries

In a blender, combine eggs, milk, water, butter, flour, and salt; blend on high until no lumps remain, scraping down sides as needed. Transfer batter to a bowl and refrigerate, covered, for at least 2 hours.

Preheat oven to 200°F (100°C).

Heat a large nonstick skillet over medium-high heat. Pour ½ cup (125 mL) batter into pan while swirling pan so batter coats the bottom. Cook for 1 to 2 minutes or until crêpe looks dry on top; carefully flip crêpe; cook for 30 seconds. Transfer to a plate, cover loosely with foil, and keep warm in oven while you repeat with remaining batter.

Spread Nutella over one quarter of each crêpe; top with strawberries. Fold crêpe in half over filling, then fold again to make a triangle.

S'MORES WAFFLES

Serves 4

Graham Cracker Crumble

4 to 6 graham crackers

Chocolate Ganache

1 cup (250 mL) semisweet chocolate
   chips or chopped chocolate

1 cup (250 mL) whipping cream

Marshmallow Fluff

1½ egg whites

1 cup (250 mL) light corn syrup

¼ tsp (1 mL) salt

1½ tsp (7 mL) pure vanilla extract

1 cup (250 mL) icing sugar

Waffles

4 waffles

Icing sugar

For the graham cracker crumble, place crackers in a plastic bag and coarsely crush by hand.

For the chocolate ganache, in a heatproof bowl set over a pot of simmering water, stir together chocolate and cream until melted and smooth. Remove from heat.

For the marshmallow fluff, in the bowl of a stand mixer fitted with the whisk attachment, combine egg whites, corn syrup, and salt. Beat on high speed for 5 minutes or until the mixture has thickened and doubled and peaks form when the whisk is lifted. Reduce speed to low, and add vanilla and icing sugar. Stir until well blended.

For the s'mores waffles, cover waffles with graham cracker crumble. Carefully spread chocolate ganache over crumble. Spread marshmallow fluff over half of each waffle. Using a kitchen blowtorch, toast marshmallow fluff. Fold waffles in half. Serve dusted with icing sugar.

When a truck's motto is "Every day I'm waffling!" you know there are some delightful fluffy Belgians coming your way, and Phi Nguyen and his crew at the Waffle Bus in Houston do not disappoint. From the waffle burgers to the waffle fries (you get the idea), waffles serve as the base for everything this gourmet truck offers.

The s'mores are just the most decadently sweet thing we've seen on the open road. Phi has solved the greatest (really only) flaw with a s'more. Once the chocolate ganache melts into the graham cracker crumble, where does all the super-oozy melted marshmallow go? The waffle serves as the ultimate edible catcher's mitt, making sure you don't miss a morsel!

TEA AND BISCUIT ICE CREAM

Makes 1 quart (1 L)

Lake Street Creamery made the most amazing ice cream! Tim Ferguson and Beth Colla had the coolest truck in Los Angeles, and I do mean cool because they made their ice cream right there in the truck. They weren't chefs; they referred to themselves as artists, and their creations were true masterpieces.

Earl Grey tea is not the most conventional ingredient when you think of ice cream, but once infused in the deep-freeze deliciousness and then mixed with butter cookie spread—guv'nor! It's hard to resist gulping this down fast, but it is the most delicious ice-cream headache you'll ever have!

3 cups (750 mL) whipping cream
¾ cup (175 mL) sugar
Pinch of salt
1 cup (250 mL) whole milk

5 Earl Grey tea bags
Speculoos cookie butter or Biscoff cookie spread

In a medium saucepan, combine 1 cup (250 mL) of the cream, sugar, and salt. Warm over medium heat until sugar is dissolved. Add remaining cream, milk, and tea bags. Reduce heat to low and simmer, stirring occasionally, until mixture is a light tan color. Remove tea bags or, if you like your tea strong, steep overnight in the refrigerator. Chill mixture before making ice cream.

Pour into ice-cream maker and freeze according to manufacturer's instructions. Transfer to a freezer-safe container. Microwave desired amount of cookie butter for about 20 seconds or until it is warm and pourable. Pour warmed cookie butter into ice cream, using a spatula to swirl it in. Freeze.

THANKS!

Pulling off a television production like *Eat St.* requires a lot of coordination and a lot of people. Producers, directors, camera operators, sound technicians, researchers, editors, and writers are just a few of the key players who work tirelessly to bring you the most delicious show on the tube! They all deserve more credit than I have room for here.

Paperny Entertainment's David Paperny, Cal Shumiatcher, and Audrey Mehler for giving me the opportunity to bring to audiences around the world a curbside view of the best food trucks on the road. Thanks for the most mouthwatering experience of my life.

Holly Gillanders at Shaw Media and everyone at Food Network Canada and Cooking Channel.

David Freeman (producer) and Amber Verville (production manager) for being the best in the biz. I will be back in Vancouver for our traditional "Japa-date" soon.

Keero Birla, Shane Geddes, and Sarah Hamblin for working their asses off in the field.

Joel Norn and all of the editors who spend untold hours putting the shows together.

My longtime friend Annelise Norohna for making me sound so good in the studio—you rock, girlgineer! (Get it? "Rock"?... Inside joke.)

Brenda Rippee for making me look good on camera and serving as our "drink concierge" when we're shooting in Los Angeles.

To the many people who have contributed to the show and/or this book on my behalf—Trevor Hodgson, Lori Kilback, Ron Barry, David Steinberg, Rick Broadhead, Susan Stafford, Monique Camenzuli, Curtis Russell, and many others whose names escape me.

Special thanks to Andrea Magyar at Penguin Group (Canada), Peter Waal (*Eat St.* producer emeritus), and my manager, Evan Adelman, who works incredibly hard for me behind the scenes and always gets me to the show on time.

And last but certainly not least, to all the wonderfully talented and entrepreneurial foodies we've met on our travels. Congratulations to all of you. Your rolling food palaces deliver incredible happiness to the streets. I know it's a cliché, but keep on truckin'!

TRUCK FINDER

RECIPE INDEX

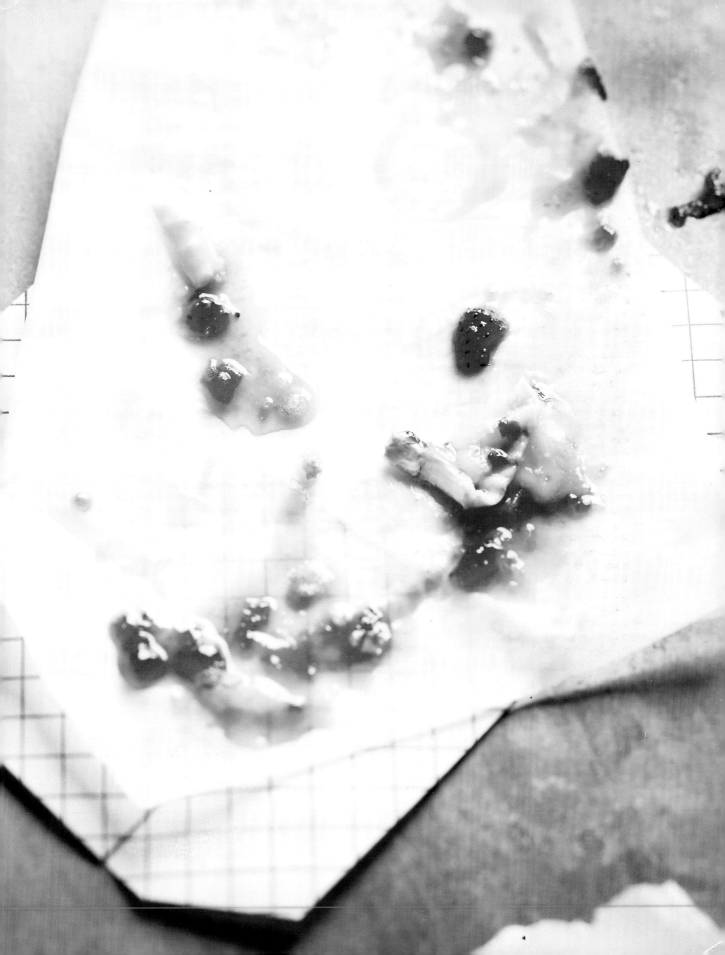

ABOUT THE AUTHOR

JAMES CUNNINGHAM is the host and associate producer of the hit TV series *Eat St.* that airs on Cooking Channel (USA) and Food Network Canada, and in more than a dozen other countries around the world. James has been featured on many national and international network television shows including *Last Comic Standing*, *Just for Laughs*, and *Comedy Now*. When not filming *Eat St.*, James keeps himself busy performing at comedy clubs, corporate shows, and with his multi-award winning youth financial literacy program, *Funny Money*.

james-cunningham.com